"One of the greatest contemporary Catholic philosophers, an intellectual concerned with politics and attentive to the unique reality of persons and things, humble before what is objective and thus opened to the truth. One great theme dominates De Corte's work the subjects of which are only apparently divergent: the vigorous denunciation of modern rationalism and an invitation to man to renew a bond with reality, without which he cannot live as a man. De Corte is above all a moralist and a philosopher of the state of crisis. As he himself declared, two subjects haunted him as a philosopher, the crisis of society and the crisis of the Church."

—**DANILO CASTELLANO**, Italian philosopher and author whose works include *L'aristotelismo cristiano di Marcel de Corte*

"One of the greatest twentieth-century masters of the counterrevolution." De Corte waged a battle of the intellect "against the current 'dis-society' of modern democracy, totalitarianism of the state, and the consumer society, and, at the same time, for the restoration of man in the fullness of his relationship to God, the world around us, and our neighbors. A brave, tireless warrior."

—**JUAN VALLET DE GOYTISOLO**, Spanish jurist and philosopher, author, among other works, of *Ideología, praxis y mito de la tecnocracia*.

"For centuries, since the moral insights of Plato and Aristotle, the virtues were considered as the heart of morality. To be good meant cultivating virtue, a training of intellect and will toward goodness which affected even the body. Morality was not conceived merely as a dry adherence to external rules but as a change of life, a true internal transformation. It is this which Marcel De Corte, with so many lively and interesting comments on contemporary society, brings to life in this series of books. They are an important contribution to what is known today as 'virtue ethics,' a cultivation of the soul as old nearly as philosophy but just as important for our moral life today."

—**THOMAS STORCK**, author, editor and translator, most recently author of *Economics: An Alternative Introduction* (XIII Books)

"The image of De Corte, obtained from his writings in *Itinéraires*, has remained with me, with his devastating analysis of: the epistemological reversal of modernity; the derangement of what is the product of this, the 'homo rationalis'; the irredeemable crisis of civilization; the corrupting character of politics founded on the 'religion of democracy,' and the tragedy which was — and still is — the crisis of the post-conciliar Church. De Corte, of an unsurpassed intellectual mettle, professed philosophical realism which is in perfect accord with his anti-modernism. The denial of an uncreated order of values leads to modernism and ends by negating tradition, religion and morality."

—**MIGUEL AYUSO**, Professor of Political Science at the Comillas Pontifical University, Madrid, and author of books on social and political topics, most recently, of *¿El pueblo contra el Estado?*

JUSTICE

Justice

MARCEL DE CORTE

Translated by Inez Fitzgerald Storck

AROUCA
PRESS

Taken from the 2nd edition published in 2019 by
Dominique Martin Morin (Poitiers, France).
This English edition also includes copious
footnotes by the translator.

ISBN: 978-1-998492-33-6

Arouca Press
PO Box 55003
Bridgeport PO
Waterloo, ON N2J 3G0
Canada
www.aroucapress.com
Send inquiries to info@aroucapress.com

Cover illustration from a print
of the Four Virtues by
Hendrick Goltzius (1558–1617)

CONTENTS

TRANSLATOR'S INTRODUCTION

WHILE MARCEL DE Corte's initial works examined more or less technical aspects of Aristotle's philosophy, after World War II he turned to a critique of society. In *On the Death of a Civilization* (Arouca, 2023) he identified causes of the decline of society: individualism, moral dissipation, consumerism, and social isolation. He discussed idealistic and materialistic philosophies undergirding these trends and ideologies objectifying workers in both capitalism and communism, both of which hold economic progress to be the overarching good. The rejection of the transcendent by some leaders and thinkers in the Church, who have compromised the truth in order to adapt to the world, has contributed to the moral degeneration of man and his rootlessness.

In *Intelligence in Danger of Death* (Arouca, 2023), De Corte offered a profound analysis of intellectual trends resulting in man's detachment from reality. A new utilitarian brand of thinking concentrates on technology and the production of consumer goods. Facts disseminated by scientists, the media, and politicians, substitute for a contemplative vision of the world based on Thomistic philosophy.

Now De Corte's volumes on the cardinal virtues do not ignore the philosophical or theological context of the virtues, but by focusing on man's failure to observe these fundamental ethical postulates, he enriches and extends his socio-political commentary to include our philosophical, political, and societal deviations.

As a Thomist, the Belgian philosopher takes as a starting point the realism of St. Thomas. He dissects activities in terms of their means and ends. The cardinal virtues illuminate our understanding of the ends we pursue in our undertakings, and the conformity of means to those ends. In contrast, situation ethics privileges a good that is sought without regard for the liceity of the means. Conscience becomes enshrined as a separate faculty, which it is not, taking the place of objective assessment of the rightness of an end and the appropriate means to achieve that end.

One of the factors crucial to this process is consideration of the common good, an important theme in De Corte's opus. He refers to the *Summa Theologiae* in this regard, "It is impossible for a man to do good unless he is properly related to the common good" (I-II, q. 96, art. 1, c.) and "Human laws should be proportionate to the common good" (I-II, q. 92, art. 1, ad 3). When the individual does not serve society by acting in consort with the common good, when society is seen as existing to serve the human being and not vice versa, then a dis-society results. This concept is so important to De Corte that he subsequently devoted an entire study to it (*De la dissociété*, R. Perrin, 2002).

When human acts are no longer ordered properly, in accord with the cardinal virtues, only technical skill, technology, remains as a driving force. The Moloch state constructed according to either the capitalist or socialist models reduces man to a cog in its machinery, the object of which is to produce material goods. While communist states, of which there were many when De Corte was writing, control production of goods through coercion, capitalist regimes privilege the interests of business through favorable tax rates, legal decisions which frequently exonerate companies with practices prejudicial to individuals and society, and failure to establish a just minimum wage. Free competition, instead of redounding, according to its theorists, to the general good of consumers and producers, results in income inequality, monopolies, exploitation of workers, and high prices.

Sohrab Ahmari in *Tyranny, Inc.: How Private Power Crushed American Liberty — and What to Do About It* (Forum Books, 2023) reports on the adverse effects of unregulated free-market capitalism on society. For example, companies facing underperformance of one of their components can make that particular enterprise a separate corporation, which is then declared bankrupt. Creditors and consumers who might have lawsuits against that spinoff firm for any wrongdoing often have no recourse. This happened in the case of Johnson & Johnson's use of asbestos in their baby power, which increased the risk of cancer. J&J neatly created a new subsidiary, which declared itself broke, unable to compensate those who developed cancer after use of the talc. As of this writing, the litigation, involving over 58,000 cases, was still ongoing. In his reportage, Ahmari examines the process whereby the government has become an appendage of big business with adverse consequences for the rights of individuals.

One may wonder if, as De Corte shows, the common good has been ignored as the individual becomes aggrandized, how he can then be reduced to a nullity. The answer is supplied: the individual self is projected onto the collectivity, which becomes another form of the self, the self writ large. "In the degree to which individuals free themselves from the supposed constraints of society and the common good, through a process of exudation they *produce* the Leviathan that shapes them in the cogs of its ruthless machinery," De Corte writes in *Prudence*. Society freed from the organizing principles of the common good and justice, its protector, becomes material to be shaped by those in power, who advance their own ideologies and interests. De Corte recalls that the work of Max Weber showed that Protestant individualism is connected to technological progress and a world bereft of a sense of the supernatural. Man becomes the future of man, in the expression of Marx. But this is man not as a member of an organic society, but of an impersonal agglomeration of individuals acceding willingly or through force to the domination of the political party or the state bureaucracy.

Those in power in the Church have contributed to this process in their failure to preserve a sense of the transcendent, to emphasize the supernatural nature of the society which the Church embodies. As they seek to implement the *aggiornamento* bitterly decried by De Corte, focusing on the here and now, and attempting to create the kingdom of God on earth, they tragically deprive society of the vision and means required to implement a just social order whose members are oriented to their final goal, union with God in heaven. By emphasizing the natural instead of the supernatural, clergy and theologians actually devalue the natural, which can only thrive with the support of reason enlightened by the cardinal virtues. In our times, this could not be more evident, as ecclesiastics in high places attempt to legitimize homosexual acts and even transgenderism. When reality is denied, the grossest distortions take hold of the minds of people, with huge consequences for individuals and society.

It suffices to examine the doctrinal system regnant in the United States, where the Church has never had much influence. Dewey's pragmatic, instrumentalist approach has been emblematic for the US, with the goal of promoting technology and scientific progress. The supernatural is rejected, replaced by humanism. The Italian philosopher Michele Federico Sciacca (1908–1975) in *La filosofia oggi* (1945) categorizes American philosophical thought as "essentially totally atheistic, even if the society in the United States calls itself Christian... [I]t is characterized by the idolatry of science, the instrument which, by means of production and technical development, will radically change humanity and provide it with every happiness...."

[O]n this point 'official' American thought is similar to Marxism. The difference between Leninism-
Marxism and pragmatic naturalistic logical positivism
lies in the lesser degree of fanaticism of Americans,
who do not make dogma out of an ideological system
as do orthodox Marxists." Eighty years after Sciacca's
incisive diagnostic, one may well ask if unrestrained
capitalism has achieved the status of dogma.

In actuality, belief in the "American way of life"
has become a religion beside which adherence to
religious denominations pales in significance, as Will
Herberg shows in *Protestant, Catholic, Jew* (1955). This
civil religion encompasses democracy, free enterprise,
individualism, and egalitarianism. The increasingly
heightened expectations of individualism have led
to the most extreme aberrations in social and moral
conduct, and the substitution of personal values for
Church doctrine. We have Catholic politicians in
both parties espousing abortion, IVF, draconian mea-
sures against immigrants and those who disagree with
foreign policy, and support for unjust wars. Versions
of the "American way of life" in contemporary dis-
society now compete with each other.

Joël Hautebert in *Cohérence de la déconstruc-
tion* (Hora Decima, 2025) explains that the roots of
dis-society and the process of what he refers to as
decivilization lie precisely in this exaggerated individualism, the very heart of modernity. This is the
source of apparently opposite ideologies, liberalism
and socialism, as well as of the movement from the
social left to the societal left, as politics has come to

focus on guaranteeing various "rights" of categories of people. Another trend Hautebert examines is the replacement of the supernatural transcendent with the secular transcendent, with society serving as a new mystical body, a characterization used by De Corte. In the new society what is absolute has been relativized, and what is relative has been absolutized, in the words of Hautebert. Readers will note that his thinking is consonant with De Corte's.

De Corte's contribution to the critique of modern society in this series lies in his focus on the consequences of the abandonment of the anchors of a just social order, respect for the common good and the cardinal virtues which support it. This is the ultimate cause of our dis-society. De Corte discusses the specific contribution of each virtue to society and what happens when the practice of the virtues is ignored.

Inez Fitzgerald Storck

I

DEFINITIONS

THE ANCIENT DEFINITION OF Ulpian,[1] *Justitia est constans et perpetua voluntas jus suum cuique tribuens,* justice is the constant and perpetual will to give each what is due him, and has a content which can never be exhausted. The division of justice into *general justice*[2] and *particular justice* is of fundamental importance. The former orders the conduct of man to others in their social relations inasmuch as they share in the common good of the community of which they are members. Particular justice orders the conduct of man to others considered as individuals with regard to the specific assets which belong to him. Of equally vital importance is the subdivision of particular justice into *distributive justice*, which renders to each person what is due him according to the place he holds in the society ruled by general justice, and *commutative justice*, which governs transactions between individuals. All that we could conceive about justice is contained in this synopsis. This is what we will attempt to demonstrate.

[1] Roman jurist (c. 170–223 or 228).
[2] Or legal justice, which "concerns what the citizen owes in fairness to the community" (CCC 2411).

II

A WARNING

I N THE REALISTIC APPROACH proper to Aristotelian and Thomistic philosophy, all actions are defined by their object. Consequently, the type of virtuous actions which are characterized as *just*, of which the *habitus*[1] is *justice*, will be defined in the same rigorously objective way. Nothing is more contrary to the modern spirit. We must then first of all ban from our vocabulary an expression commonly used today, "the demands of justice," which delights politicians and lay and ecclesiastical clergy of every stripe: its subjective connotations are clear. What indeed is a demand if not as the dictionary defines it, "what man requires as necessary for the fulfillment of his needs, desires, and aspirations"? Now, since the only man who can make demands is the individual, the person considered as the basis of an action, in short, the human *subject*, then "justice" taken to be the fulfillment of a need can only be the product of subjectivism. The "demands" of justice are, in fact, as experience shows only too well, the *demands of the self* who refuses to submit to the *reality* which we call *justice* and

[1] Habit, *habitus* being the singular and plural of the noun.

who substitutes a *mental construct* drawn from his appetites and passions.

There is no word more charged with passion than *justice*. Each person demands it according to the *representation* he has formed of it, which immediately reveals his lack of conformity to reality, without even taking into account the emotive potential it is loaded with, which gives it a specious content. This volatile justice is not measured to its object, but to the subject who lays claim to it and who bloats his claims to the bursting point, summoning to his aid the moral strictures allegedly outraged in his person.

Indeed, one of the most-neglected facts about the modern spirit intoxicated with subjectivism is the classic distinction between the object of the moral virtues other than justice and the object of justice itself. The object of fortitude and temperance, along with their related virtues, is the moral *subject* himself: their aim is to impart rectitude to the irascible and concupiscible passions of the subject in order to establish them according to the golden mean regarding the subject. This golden mean will differ from one individual to the next. The properly moral virtues perfect the actual subject, the moral agent. They ensure the excellence of the person. They perfect the concrete human individual. They straight away elevate their author and source. This is why the intense, exclusive cultivation of the moral virtues properly speaking, such as fortitude and temperance, can lead to pride, self-sufficiency, or even puffed-up pomposity, in the subject in whom they are seated.

It can drive the person to focus only on himself and his own glory. Witness the stoic, the athlete of virtue, his eyes constantly fixed on himself, on his greatness, to the exclusion of everything else: "Myself alone, and that suffices."[2]

Without justice, which enables the subject to get out of himself, which always relates to others (*ad alium*), the rectitude of which is always found in the object, the measure of which is always a thing (or a service or action) independent of and distinct from the involved parties (a sum of money to be paid back, for example), morality will remain a prisoner of subjectivism and the consequences which follow in its wake: the autonomy of the subject and his denial of any rule other than one deriving its content and governing power from him alone. This would mean the collapse of all social life. Law would have no objective basis. Justice would flee from an iron century which would reduce it to the sheer will of man. It would generate a pseudo-society in which each member would infallibly become both the tyrant and parasite of others.

[2] A reference to the words of Medea in Corneille's play (*Médée*, 1635) emphasizing her inviolability when she is beset with opposition from every side.

III
JUSTICE, A REALISTIC VIRTUE

S ARISTOTLE AND ST. Thomas have so clearly perceived, in every just act an *object* is always interposed between the subject having a right and the subject having an obligation: this trans-subjective *reality* evaluates the right of the former and the obligation of the latter, independently of the good or bad intentions of the persons involved. Whatever the inner dispositions or state of mind of the parties concerned, only their actions matter and are termed just because they are defined by something external; they are a function of something exterior (*res exterior*) to them. One could charge justice thus conceptualized with "formalism" or "legalism," but this comes from a complete misunderstanding of the eminent place it occupies in the choir of virtues.

Justice, then, is weighted with a twofold ballast of objective reality: first, the *other person*, one of the two parties in the relationship where justice comes into play, and second, the *matter* involved in the transaction, which serves as an intermediary between the two parties in the relationship. *To do the just thing (id quod justum est) towards others, such is the work of justice.* Justice connects one person to another in a *social* relationship sealed by a *reality* independent of passions, which are always subjective, and through which the obligation of justice can be impaired on the part of either the person to whom something is owed or the party which must repay what is owed. Without this second objective reality, the matter, there would be no connection between one person and another; there would be no social relationship. The matter of the transaction in the relationship is the basis of it, and not the parties involved. In other words, there exists between them *something* lent and thus due. There is only a real society among people if they share in *realities* of every kind: material, moral, intellectual, spiritual, independent of any subjective attitude they may have concerning these, which are objectively, that is, in a material sense, imposed on them. Actual society is not established by the decisions of persons within it, but on objective, material realities common to them, preceding their respective desires, which for better or worse must be conformed to these realities. What each of us receives from others at the moment of our birth and during the course of our existence is incomparably superior to what we could give to them or what we actually render to them, and in no way depends on a free choice of ours: beyond *life* which we receive from the original, fundamental group which is the family, and which we pass on to others when we found a home of our own, there are shelter, food, and a degree of comfort

superior to that of animals. In addition, through families brought together in a community which transcends and embraces them we are provided, not from any free choice of ours, with material well-being and all the inestimable treasures of the state and civilization, which we are responsible for maintaining and transmitting to others.

This realism, this *specificity*,[1] in a social relationship, visible and so to speak tangible in the duality of persons where one individual has a connection with another (for example, a certain sum of money put temporarily at the disposition of one of them which must be repaid to the other according to the demands of *particular* justice), is also characteristic of the relationship which each human person has with the society in which he lives, through which he is recognized as a servant of the polity and of all those who are part of it. This relationship is ruled by *general* justice, which is concerned with the good of the community, the *common good* to which each individual is ordered; he must contribute to the common good of the community as well as to that of its members. This common good encompasses innumerable benefits, essentially *everything which unites people to each other*. While the *matter* regulated by particular justice can be determined, referring to a specified quantity, the matter governed primarily by general justice has no boundaries. The definition of justice which St. Thomas inherited from the Digest

[1] *Chosisme* in French.

of Justinian,[2] "a constant and perpetual will to render to each person his due," has a radiant clarity when it comes to *particular* justice and the *specific* goods which *personally* concern us and which involve other *persons* in the *real, objective sphere* where justice holds sway, where matters are clearly defined, limited, quantified, with this or that quantity, no more no less. The object, matter, or service which determines the obligation of one party and the right of the other is fixed within precise limits. As soon as it no longer concerns the "other" taken as a person, but the "other" considered socially (*alius in communi*), as a member of society, then the common good, which constitutes the actual context, the *medium rei*, for each of us and the society we are a part of, lacks the same clarity, as it is quite wide-ranging. Similarly unclear are the obligation which each must render to the community and the right of the community to require each of us to fulfill this obligation. Such is the paradox of general justice. Its reality is not apparent due to its vast content: it has the same universal breadth as the object of the intellect and the will, which is not easily grasped.

[2] Compendium of Roman law compiled by order of the Byzantine emperor Justinian I in 530–533.

IV
THE COMMON GOOD

E ARE CONFRONTED with a reality which defies our understanding, so much does it surpass our intellectual capacity, a reality characterized by the ancients, in their ardor and humility, as "divine." From the most basic community, the family, to the comprehensive community which is the world, including the many intervening communities, one of which, the political society of which we are members, is the most laden with bounty for us and, in addition, puts its stamp on us, we are integrated into a "Great Being," as August Comte termed it,[1] which both constitutes us and transcends us. How could the part observe and understand the modalities of the whole, of which it is a part and into which it is subsumed? How could it assess the various common goods which all these communities bring with them, the bounty of which makes us committed to them?

---

[1] A reference to the "Great Being of Humanity," considered by the French philosopher and mathematician Comte (1798–1857) as taking the place of a divinity in the secular humanism he professed. A surprising reference on the part of De Corte, whose conception of the "Great Being" is obviously different from Comte's.

Let us consider *existence* once again, the greatest of goods, the root of all the others, for which we are indebted to our parents, and which connects us to the hierarchy of common goods of which the family is the repository. It is not out of an empty romantic lyricism that Lamartine sings "the family is the world in minia-ture."[2] It is in one way undoubtedly the sphere of the private par excellence, but in another, more lofty sense, the family, not the isolated individual, represents the microcosm where the world had its beginning. Isn't it in the family that we receive the common good of language, "honor of men,"[3] the source of all the others, which establishes our first human, intelligible connections with others? Isn't it a sort of cultural matrix for us which succeeds that of the mother who bore us? Isn't it the means through which we are ini-tiated into the progression of lofty and salutary laws which permeate the created universe, spoken of by Edgar Allan Poe?[4] Isn't it through the mediation of its discipline and rules that we are ordered to all other common goods and initiated into the duties incum-bent on us which are themselves rooted in the nature of things? Isn't the Father of gods and men invoked by Homer, the heavenly Father to whom the Christian prays, reflected in the earthly father as Plato implies?

[2] "Neuvième époque" in *Jocelyn* (1836). Alphonse de Lamartine (1790–1869), considered to be the first French romantic poet, also wrote novels, plays and works of history.

[3] From "La Pythie" in *Charmes ou poèmes* (1926), by the French poet and essayist Paul Valéry (1871–1945).

[4] Poe expounds on this notion in a lengthy prose-poem, *Eureka* (1848).

If this is the case with the seminal common good, the family, what must be the superior common goods into whose sphere we enter in the course of our life and whose riches penetrate to our inmost being, compelling us, if we observe general justice which governs them, to preserve them, strengthen them, and communicate them to others? It is in the family that we perceive the inexhaustible truth of the ancient metaphysical adage *bonum est diffusivum sui*, goodness is diffusive of itself; the characteristic of good is to spread itself abroad and give of itself; the good is everything that creates unity. Thanks to the biologically exclusive nature of the family, we experience as it were its warm physical presence. If we open the eyes of our *intellect*, we feel the reflection of its light in the larger communities to which our birth destines us and commits us.

Höderlin thus had reason to affirm that "birth is in large part decisive"[5] when it comes to the common good, which precedes our individual existence onto which it impresses its life-sustaining form, spreading its boundless influence until it establishes our being in its very essence. Moreover, the denial of the common good, which is accompanied by the withdrawal of the person into himself, is always a mutilation, resulting in *any and every illusion without a single exception*, about ourselves, the world, and God, similar to an amputated limb which creates its phantom presence. In order to alleviate the anguish brought about by

[5] Friedrich Höderlin (1770–1843), German poet and philosopher. The citation is from his poem "The Rhine" (1808).

this loss, the individual has no other recourse than to create *another* "common good" *out of nothing*, starting with the subjective alone, stripped of its inborn connection to others and to the world, which will always retain its illusory, deceptive nature, in spite of the most dissembling or blatant attempts to incarnate it into existence. The pseudo-communities constructed on the foundation of the individual or collective self are only entities denuded of real existence in which, for those who dream up these communities, phantasms conceal the terribly real existence, unobserved by their victims, of prosthetic devices more "life-like" in appearance and more constraining than our natural relations with others in the diverse societal groups where we find ourselves. Examples are the herd-like movement of groups of *hippies*, or, at the other extreme of the current dis-society, the bureaucratic and police systems of totalitarian states. The denial of the common good is freeing in the imagination but harshly enslaving in reality.

It cannot be otherwise. The distinctive feature of the common good is that it is not depleted when it is shared. The love of a father or mother is not exhausted when it is directed to a greater number of children. Masterpieces of art are not impoverished when they are viewed by a host of connoisseurs in each generation. But the defining characteristic of the self cut off from its constitutive relation to others, to the world, to God, is to be bled dry straight away because it no longer imbibes of the realities which sustain it. The replacement products which it manufactures in its solitude in order to fill it are of a wearisome uniformity. Artificial social paradises are monotonous. Nothing is more like a utopia than another utopia. To escape from the revulsion if not horror which is covertly provoked by every attempt (for that matter quickly aborted) to incarnate a utopia in history, it must be repudiated, then another adopted, just as repulsive, then yet another, ad infinitum. The permanent revolution in which contemporary humanity is steeping is a substitute for the common good whose existence it does not even suspect, so much as it been infected with "personalism."

Alexis de Tocqueville had already observed this in 1848: "Here is the French revolution starting anew, for it is always the same."[6] There where it forcibly brings together human atoms, the bureaucratic and police machinery is condemned to stasis, and the most rigid of orthodoxies. The least change would demolish the monolith. The modern revolution preserves the pseudo-society which it engenders like a mummy. It is incapable of spiritual or intellectual progress because it transmits nothing. Material progress, except with regard to weapons, is forbidden to it: economic abundance would be a kind of common good! It is left with only more and more coercion. The Prague spring[7] was very brief. In fact, nothing in a totalitarian system can change without calling into question its very existence.

[6] From his private journal on the revolution of 1848, published posthumously in *Souvenirs* (1893). De Tocqueville (1805–1859) was a French diplomat and political philosopher.

[7] A liberalizing reform movement in communist Czechoslovakia brutally crushed by the Soviet Union in 1968, several months after it began.

V

THE COMMON GOOD, UNIFYING AND ENRICHING

THE INEXHAUSTIBLE NATURE of the common good of which general justice is the guardian is further manifested in the almost infinite multiplicity of modes of bringing together the members of a living society in space and time, where the gradual deposits left by these modes through the millennia clearly constitute this common good. The ancients in this regard compare the relationship among members of the state to the state itself with that of the parts of a whole to the whole. The common good is for them the coming together of all the parts which constitute the whole, with all the aspects of this union working in concert. It is a form of ordering, the reciprocal ordering of the parts among themselves, which enables their interactions, their mutual aid, their complementarity; whatever fosters this mutual relationship belongs to the domain of the common good. Thus, the common good must not be represented as a substantive whole extrinsic to the parts which constitute it, existing by and for itself. The common good is not the good of the whole considered as a kind of singular entity. It is the good of the whole which happens to come into existence, which respects the significant differences among its parts: in this case, human beings, the diversity of their characters and their countless activities, the differences which characterize them individually, their specific personalities. Now the concrete situations of human beings are inexhaustible and defy all description. They fluctuate considerably, changing at every moment. The social whole is not only made up of its parts, but also of their activities, of which the number, variety, and personal interactions defy any exhaustive analysis. Every act informed by general justice is accomplished *hic et nunc*[1] and is embedded in circumstances such that another act, seemingly similar, coming from the same person, would never be identical to it. The common good is made up of countless deposits of sediment, or if you prefer another metaphor, of tiny corals which in the course of centuries eventually built up the Great Barrier Reef in the warm waters of the south. The lives of people established in a society are made up of all kinds of interactions, infinite in number, of which the accumulation, organic continuity, and ever-increasing cohesion unite the parts of the whole to a greater and greater degree in a harmoniously ordered community—which does not mean perfect! —where multifaceted interrelations, actualized in the very existence of the community and in all the goods

[1] Here and now.

it brings with it, from the material level, of lesser
importance, to the spiritual level, of greater importance, are the common good of those who are members of the community. Such is the object which each
person is obligated to be heedful of and which each
in his own way is obliged to render to others as their
due in the name of general justice.

We never tire of repeating that the prodigious variety of the common good never ceases to bring about
unity because each human action which contributes
to it by adhering to it while implementing it and
implementing it while adhering to it has no other
outcome than maintaining and strengthening unity
among members of the community. The common
good is: *everything which unites, including those not
belonging to the society*, which gathers people together;
relations of every kind which they form generation
after generation; the immeasurable number of *actual
experiences*, accumulated in their life in society, perpetuated beyond their brief existence. On the contrary,
according to the apt expression of Claudel, "evil does
not create"[2]: it only places side by side those whom it
appears to united together in its work of destruction.
In fact, evil renders asunder. As an ancient father of
the Church said, through original sin man is *separated from himself and from others*. We do not err
when we say of evil that it *tears asunder*. That is
literally true. Evil is *everything that separates*.

[2] Paul Claudel (1868–1955), eminent French dramatist, poet,
essayist and diplomat. The citation is from his *Journal*, vol. II,
1933–1955, published in 1969.

VI

VARIOUS MODES OF RELATIONSHIP TO THE COMMON GOOD

F IT IS TRUE THAT THE COMMON good is the object of general justice, a virtue concerned with the will or rational appetite and seated in man, a concrete being living in society, it follows that his responsibility in this regard is a strictly a personal matter *and will differ from person to person* according to the intellectual and volitional capability with which he is endowed, and, as well, to the objective character of his acts. Contrary to egalitarianism, rampant in modern politics, it is important to affirm in the strongest possible terms, since the very security of the human being inasmuch as he is a social animal is at risk, that there is no society, and consequently no common good inherent in society, without the existence of felicitous, fruitful *inequalities* among its members. The entity of society is in fact only a cloth woven out of relations and interchanges among people, which engender unity. Inequality among them is a presupposition. One does not unite identical beings. There would not be the least communication among them since absolutely equal persons would have absolutely nothing to discuss. Identical persons merge into just one entity or rather they settle down, each one closed in on himself, side by side with the others, to form nothing more than a scattered multiplicity of monads with no connection to each other.

Only where there are differences can there be unity. The strong lend their strength to the weak, but weakness, thus supported, itself becomes strength, so that unity and the common good are enhanced on both sides. So it is in all other areas, and especially in the sphere of civilization: the initiated receives benefits from the initiator and proves himself able to initiate others, thus enriching the common good with his contribution and strengthening the union which establishes it. The void immediately gives rise to plenitude, always ready to be poured out, as with communicating vessels,[1] so that the tutelary, protective, salutary, succoring, collaborative and convergent inequalities (the constant *physical* presence of which Maurras describes for us in the remarkable pages of his *Politique naturelle*[2]) order the only true *equalities* which all authentic social life manifests: those concerning mutual assistance, where the contribution

[1] Containers connected by tubes positioned below the level of the liquid in them, which then settles at the same level in all the containers.

[2] The title given by Maurras to a preface to his book *Mes idées politiques* (1937). Charles Maurras (1868–1952) was a French writer, politician and poet who advocated monarchism, integralism, and a counterrevolution.

of each person multiplies the common good, which benefits all and which would have been to the advantage of no one if each person had been walled up in an initial chimerical equality. Unity makes strength, according to the national motto of Belgians: it enhances the life of the whole, and, consequently, the life of all the parts, even the most minuscule. Which is preferable, to be in one's imagination the exact equal of others in a mythical society or to be equal in a certain manner, that is, analogously, in a way which corresponds to the part, in a visible, concrete community? In an actual society, where the common good prevails over harmful divisiveness, the lowliest of the members has his place, secured *in the same way* as that of the most important member.

Here also the family, cell of every community as well as its reflection, bears witness: isn't the child at the breast, who gives nothing and receives everything, actually part of the family *in the same way* as a grandparent who is rich in experience? In spite of and because of his obvious *inequality*, isn't he on an *equal* footing with the grandparent? The common good realized in the close familial union is their point of convergence: the lines are different, yet they arrive at the *same* point. The structure of the family, hierarchical with regard to biology and mode of conduct, is transposed onto other, larger communities. In all places the common good in some fashion equalizes the inequalities necessary for the formation of the familial bond, inequalities which are inscribed in the very nature of the persons it brings together.

It goes without saying that the common good of
the familial community imposes different obligations
on the members of the hierarchy which compose
it: children and parents. It is normal, and willed by
nature, that the father and mother sacrifice themselves
for their children and feel more intensely than these
that they are responsible for the common good which
is perpetuated through their descendants. The expression *unnatural* parents shows clearly that the refusal
to comply with general justice is in this case felt as
a violation of a law immanent in the very nature of
man to which one *must* submit in order *to be* a man.
To what acts of devotion hasn't the concept of "the
honor of the family name" brought some parents?
In every society whose soul is the common good it is
the leaders who are the first ones exposed to dangers:
their position in the hierarchy puts them into the
most direct contact with the whole and, consequently,
with the ensemble of parts contained in this whole,
which it is important to protect against the menace
of disunity: the summit protects the base. Louis
XIV wrote to his grandson that his mission was to
safeguard the common good, for which purpose a
monarch is born. The plume of Henry IV[3] presented
quite another picture from the flight abroad of the
"representatives of the people," which we witnessed
in the distressing spectacle of 1940![4] The higher one

[3] In the Wars of Religion, during the battle of Ivry (1590) Henry
IV of France wore white feathers on his helmet to identify himself, so that he could serve as a rallying point.
[4] Several French leaders fled when the Nazis invaded France,

is in the hierarchy of any society, the more he experiences the common good of its members as an *object* of fundamental necessity for the human being and the only proper *object* apt for assessing the scope of their existence: *being* is essentially *being with*, with each of the members of a given community, with all of them, with the entire group.

some, such as Charles de Gaulle, to participate in the activities of the resistance abroad.

VII
THE COMMON GOOD
OF THE STATE

T FOLLOWS THAT IN AN ORGANIC society close to the sources of life, such as the family, the common good is understood in a straightforward, prereflexive manner as the best good for the subject, since as he pursues it, his life is fulfilled. The law which each being in the world bears within, *to become what he is,*[1] is applied to man not as an individual separate from others, but as a part bound by both birth and temperament to the other parts of each community he belongs to. It is indisputable that the good of the family is for each of its members the good of all the other members and not something one of them would jealously keep for himself. We can put our finger here, so to speak, on the mysterious nature of the common good which just one word expresses, *unity.* Every house divided against itself will fall: the permanence of its existence

[1] Recalling the injunction to "become what you are" of the Greek lyric poet Pindar (c. 518 BC–c. 438 BC) in his Second Pythian Ode, and taken up over the centuries by scholars and the popular culture. It is the title of the biography De Corte wrote with his wife of their son who died young.

is a function of *everything that unites its members*. This is why the common good of the family lies in unity—and everything material and spiritual that unity brings with it, which each of its members *owes* to the others and vice versa. To say of a family that it is unified means that each of its members enjoys the greatest of goods.

What is natural at the level of the family takes on other characteristics at higher levels of society where the power of instinct does not have the same spontaneity or potential to come into play. Also, Aristotle and St. Thomas who only had before them one kind of domestic society, in which each member, wife, children, menservants and maids, was considered as the very extension of the head of the family, go so far as to say that there is strictly speaking no justice nor common good in this exclusively private domain, since there is no actual relationship with others: the master of the household is always in the presence of himself. So that there could be *someone other than the self*, we have to go beyond the biological level of animal drives to arrive at the level of reason and its imperatives.

In the Middle Ages as in antiquity, the distinction between the private and public spheres was strict. The threshold both separating them and connecting them could not be crossed without harm to the human being. If the private sphere encroaches on the public domain, man falls under the tyranny of one individual, and the private sphere if it is encompassed by the public domain is crushed by the tyranny of all. To escape from this dilemma and avoid becoming

prey to the fear of finding himself isolated when he
encounters others taken either as individuals or a collectivity, man must be able to have access to one or the
other of these superimposed spheres. The existence
of the restricted community which is the family is
not enough to protect him. Only the state can, like
the family, enable him to escape from solitude, and
to go from *life* and the mere prolongation of life to
access to *a better life, properly human*, disposed to
make room for others in the universal sense of the
term. The conflict between persons who are *strangers*
to each other can only be surmounted when the fear
that arises dissipates and groups of people appear to
each other with a countenance made serene by an act
of practical reason. This, by acting as an extension
of the powerless animal instinct, creates with them
bonds seated in the *specific* nature of man as he is
defined. The domain of the private (family, household,
business, agriculture, trades and professions, etc....)
is where the continuity of life and significant interchanges are renewed and maintained. The nature
of man is not content with just that. Because he is
endowed with language and reason, the human being
refers to this place of important interactions, where
his natural sociability is fulfilled and thrives within
a civilization termed the *state*, as a perfect society,
in spite of all its historical imperfections and flaws,
because it is the work of reason and will, perfections
possessed by man. Without the help of the intellect
and a hunger for the good, both abundantly present
in man and enabling him to embrace, strengthen and

elevate the efforts of a flagging social instinct, he would remain at the level of a higher animal in which the awareness of unity is sufficient to maintain the union itself, but proves unable to elevate it further. The transcendence of the intellect is only evident in the state which it creates and which causes it to flourish. In the domain of the private, the state is subordinate to the urgent requirements of life and survival of which it becomes the instrument. The desire to live better and to have access to goods of a more eminent value can only be fulfilled in a society where exchanges of words, ideas, opinions, judgments, inventions, arts and sciences, creations of the mind which due to the very realities which they convey are at once the causes and effects of the actual union which they establish in the wills of the members of the community.

Here art adds to nature, and is a continuation of it, deepening it, amplifying it, through the establishment of institutions and promulgation of laws which encourage people to fulfill themselves as perfectly as possible and to come together for a more noble purpose than the perpetuation of biological life, that is, *for a virtuous life*, for an existence in which each person, in accord with his capabilities and gifts, can make use of the potential and virtues which he has insofar as he is a man. From this perspective, social and rational animals are one and the same, as is proven by their common masterpiece, *civilization*.

Our age, ravaged by the twin excesses of individualism and collectivism, has lost even the memory of

the ultimate end of the state, the work of men, an
end which is one with the state and establishes it as
a perfect society, able to help its members through
their union with it to go from looking for the *means*
of sustenance necessary for the maintenance and prop-
agation of life to searching for specifically human
ends. We are no longer aware that man is incapable
of leading a virtuous life on his own, and that the
hermit in the desert or the stylite on his pillar communicates intensely with God, and, through Him,
with the world: "Mine are the heavens and mine is
the earth, and all created things," cries St. John of
the Cross[2] at the final stage of his mystical ascent.

"Man living alone is either a beast or a god": this
aphorism of Aristotle's[3] illuminates our destiny.
To do without cooperation with others, to strive
in total independence for the perfection which is
proper to us, to experience social life as alienation,
as a loss of one's essence, and as an encroachment
on our complete autonomy, to proclaim moreover
that "hell is other people"[4] consequently implies
that society, without which, nevertheless, man cannot exist, must be *entirely* the work of individuals
working independently.

This is a round square. How could completely
independent individuals with no prior relationships
create among themselves a network of relationships
other than imaginary ones? It is impossible for man

[2] Free citation from his "Sayings of Light and Love" (n.d.).
[3] A loose quotation from *Politics*.
[4] From Sartre's play *Huis clos* (1944).

to draw his existence out of nothing, and to construct the *social* via the *individual*. The personalist, communitarian state is a myth, a chimera of disembodied intellectuals *bombinans in vacuo*,[5] which only exists in the mind which conceives it, a purely verbal projection of an ego contemplating itself in its own mirror and mentally identifying itself with others.

Since man thus amputated from his congenital, ontological relationship to others can in no way dispense with society, it will never be more than an arbitrary, artificial construct imposed from without onto separate components which it forcibly joins together. Totalitarian collectivism is the inevitable counterpart of individualism, and "socialism with a human face" is only a dream which obscures the harsh reality of a system based on physical coercion, the indispensable prosthetic which replaces the natural social bonds which have disappeared.

One only creates the *social* in the full meaning of the word by means of the *social* in the rudimentary sense of the term. One only creates what is *institutional* with what is *natural*, and, since the natural is found in the first place in the community of the family, itself rooted in biological life, a state worthy of the name will always be, according to the expression of Bodin,[6] inherited from Aristotle,[7] an assembly of *families* associated among themselves in order to

[5] Buzzing in a vacuum.
[6] Jean Bodin (c. 1530–1596), French political philosopher who believed that families were the basic unit of the state.
[7] *Politics.*

go from merely *living* to *living better*. The public does not differ from the private as its opposite and antagonist, but is something correlative to it, like a superior with regard to his subordinate.

In this respect the state, creation of the people, is just as much a natural community as the family. It is even more so since it endows with intellect and will the impulses towards unity manifested throughout life and multiplies almost to infinity the benefits of rudimentary associations among people.

VIII
THE CAPITAL IMPORTANCE OF BIRTH

THE RATIONAL DESIRE FOR well-being and a perfected condition which motivates man to establish the state is based on *birth* in the widest sense of the term, referring to the family of origin and the place of birth, factors which do not depend on human liberty. Positive law, created by the will of man, is grafted onto the natural law, which does not come under its jurisdiction. The institutions, the product of human deliberation, that are most certain means of providing the societies they direct and their members with a happy life are those that cultivate, arouse, and increase the feeling of living and working for each other's good in the family. Institutions are derived from the natural tendency to provide mutual assistance and create unity, from a spontaneous subordination of the part to the whole which characterizes the society of the family. This tendency is, however, sublimated, strengthened, and enriched by enlightened, intelligent effort.

The history of these institutions shows this: those designed theoretically in the minds of men, the "written constitutions," Joseph de Maistre spoke of,[1] cast into the dust of a "dis-society," are almost always creators of disequilibrium, while regimes established on the basis of the slow sedimentation of mores, customs, and common practices are, as a result of an equally slow empirical process of organization and rational legislation, shown to be reservoirs and providers of long-lasting social energies.

[1] De Maistre (1753–1821) was a philosopher and diplomat from Savoy. See his *Essai sur le principe générateur des constitutions politiques* (1814), in which he inveighs against constitutions drawn up through deliberation, and not derived from customs and traditions.

IX
THE FRAGILITY
OF SOCIAL BONDS

HE EXISTENCE OF PROPERLY human social relations is extremely fragile. What the intellect adds to the reliable, solid associations born from life, far from resulting in a better life and strengthening natural unity, always ends up with disappointing results, if the institutional implementation of these mental constructions is not subject to *validation from experience, which, in social affairs, is only supplied by the past.* Here there is no point of reference other than tradition and its lessons. *Historia magistra vitae.*[1] History teaches us that there were happy, prosperous societies and reveals the causes of their decline. "I call utopia," says the Spanish poet, "whatever did not occur in the course of Roman history." And in the last century a member of the House of Commons in the course of a difficult debate warned his colleagues that there was no solution to a political problem not found in Thucydides.[2]

---

[1] History is the teacher of life, an expression used by Cicero in *De Oratore*.
[2] Athenian historian and general (c.460–400 BC).

Nature, left to itself, only yields brambles and thorns; nature when violated by man is transformed into a desert; but nature, assisted and elevated by human politics, yields good fruit.

The successful intervention of man in the formation of social bonds derives from various factors the importance of which cannot be underestimated. For a robust, enduring union, it is not sufficient for institutions to be in keeping with nature; that is, legal concepts of the "poetic"[3] intellect should be the work of an expert knowledgeable about natural laws, whose respect for them ensures a stable, deep-rooted foundation. It is further necessary that nature itself, which imposes unity in its rudimentary form, not be distorted by the interference of the human intellect and will. The intellect can be correct or false, and the will can be upright or deviant. The designs of nature can be heeded or contravened. Moreover, one can have a sound intellect but an aberrant will. Then, since nothing is willed unless it is first known and nothing is known except from its causes and, ultimately, from its final Cause, the fate of the state will depend on its institutions insofar as they are based on a concept of man, the world, and their Principle, on a metaphysics and natural religion implicitly and fundamentally conformed in their basic inspiration to reality.

In fact, we must arrive at the modern era to see states appear on the scene of history which are unencumbered by any apparent relation to metaphysics

---

[3] In the sense of the Greek verb *poiein, to make, fashion, construct or produce a work external to the agent.*

or religion, but then again, we must come to the same era to observe without a doubt that "societies" governed by the principle of secularism are unstable: there is no contemporary "society" which does not suffer from the onslaught of the most varied forms of opposition and whose existence is not perpetually called into question. The "permanent revolution"[4] is a myth inasmuch as it is the denial of the natural union among men, and is thus incapable of ensuring their happiness. Yet this chimera is a reality inasmuch as it undermines, sometimes with silent, furtive attacks, other times through volcanic conflagrations, the social edifice which is not devoted to the common good.

A society is formed by alluvial layers of *acts of justice*, and what is the opposite of acts — the *word*, dream, utopia, ideology — relentlessly undermines it. "Not everyone who says to Me, 'Lord, Lord' will enter the kingdom of heaven, but only the one who does the will of My Father in heaven" says the Gospel [Matt. 7:21]. By the same token, it is not those who cry out on the stages of all the crossroads "Dialogue, dialogue!" who will remake the social fabric, rent apart, but those who, spontaneously and unobtrusively through little acts of *real* mutual assistance, will fill in the breaches.

---

[4] According to Marx, this refers to continuous revolutionary activity until a goal (socialism or communism) is reached.

X

SOCIETY AND RELIGION

N THIS REGARD, THE CHRISTIAN religion, whatever judgment might be made of its truth, is the only one which has instructed people to observe the natural law, which prescribes solidarity as the source of every community. When St. Paul enjoins Christians to provide mutual assistance and to bear each other's burdens and so fulfill the law of Christ [Gal. 6:2], he only takes to a higher level an observation of the wisdom of the ages:

> If your neighbor has died
> The burden falls on you.[1]

The warning of the fabulist is the expression of a law which governs every natural community and permeates every authentic institution: when the father of a family dies, the mother or the eldest son, if he is of age, shoulders the burden. The old-timer Nisard[2] observed that there was scarcely a home, even a humble one, where the diocesan catechism and the *Fables*

---

[1] "Le cheval et l'âne," by French fabulist Jean de la Fontaine (1621–1695).
[2] Désiré Nisard (1806–1888), French journalist and literary critic. He discusses the importance of La Fontaine in his *Histoire de la littérature française* (1844–1861), vol. 3.

of La Fontaine could not be found. Christianity is
the only revealed religion which obligates people to
strengthen the bonds already formed among them by
nature and which, while informing the institutions
which they have created, shows them that grace, far
from abolishing nature, elevates it. With good reason
a positivist like Maurras could proclaim the benevo-
lence of Christianity.

No society exists without a system of religious
beliefs which strengthens the precariousness of social
relations and serves as its cornerstone, now transcendent and unshakable, shining forth in the behavior
of its members. Over the centuries, the establishment of a state has always been accompanied by a
religious invocation to the Immutable: The American constitution was proclaimed in the name of the
Most Holy Trinity,[3] just as Athens was placed under
the protection of Pallas and Rome under Janus and
Minerva. Up until the French Revolution, all pagan
peoples invoked gods as they promulgated laws, while
Christian peoples invoked God. For all of these it
was a matter of safeguarding social ties, by definition
precarious, securing them with an unbreakable bond.
In every society which aspires to endure, there must
exist between citizens and succeeding generations a
cohesive force which transcends their brief existence
and which their wills, fixed in time with its ravages,
cannot themselves pass on to them. According to
ancient moralists, the love of country is connected

[3] De Corte could have been thinking of the Irish constitution
here, as the American constitution is not Christian.

to the virtue of piety, the fervent love for what is beyond human life in its brief span.

Man is, in effect, according to Nietzsche's expression, the only animal that can make promises.[4] How could he enter into a vibrant and permanent relationship with others and assure them of his fidelity beyond all the vicissitudes that might affect the relationship if Another, invisible and immutable, were not among them in order to confirm their mutual faith? Every union willed to be constant in some way lifts man up from time to eternity. This was known by the ancients, who called politics, or the art of enabling human societies to endure, divine. The state is the place of convergence for the wills of people rendered constant by means of a common good which obligates them and transcends them, because in the last analysis it is connected to the universal Common Good which is God.

This is why secular "societies" are religious in their own way. Whether they are democratic or totalitarian, they substitute the worship of Man, or whatever other Entity in capital letters, for the worship of gods and God. This is why there exist and will always exist so many caricatures of the state: the idols made by man to imitate the Divinity are innumerable. For them to proliferate it is enough for people to replace the state grafted onto nature with a state up in the clouds with its ideologies. Since they no longer have among themselves an actual common good which

---

[4] See his *Genealogy of Morality* (1887), vol. 2.

is the *object* of their wills, they are constrained to conceive of a *substitute*, to the point where the strongest and shrewdest ego imposes his own will on all the rest, under the guise of a nebulous philosophy which stupefies the intellect and prevents it from acting on its own behalf: a decree is issued, but one which arouses herding instincts among the people and hurls them into servitude. The *cult* of personality which runs rampant in all democratic, liberal, and totalitarian regimes, whose roots are impossible to extirpate, bears witness to this.

The relationship between the art of politics and nature, and between intelligence and life (common to people and animals) tends, despite all disavowals, to become reconstituted, *but at the lowest level*: intellectually, at the level of the imagination, and physically, at the level of the conditioned reflex. Since no quarter is given to the reality of the principle of causality nor to natural religion, which it informs, people in their folly hastily erect a mystical and mystifying construct in which the degradation to which they are condemned by nature, which they have offended, forces them into a corner as the construct replaces the now-disappeared legitimate sacralization of the social. This is the story of every form of socialism and collectivism: they are only maintained thanks to human credulity, gullible with regard to the illusory and prone to make a silk purse out of a sow's ear. The proof of this is the overvaluation of the future, the privileged place for every mirage, which we are currently witnessing. "Let them be conquered by idealism," said Lenin cynically of the numberless gullible members of the modern intelligentsia, exiles from reality and makers of illusions.

We could continue almost indefinitely in this vein. It is the modern world, inasmuch as it is modern, where what is current, new, and ephemeral has taken the place of traditional wisdom, that we must indict here. The modern world has denied the primacy of the contemplative intellect, which is governed by conformity to *what is* and receptive to unchangeable truths of a *metaphysical* order, and it reaps the consequences. It cannot guarantee the least stability to social institutions, and, even worse, it cannot even conceive of respect for the common good, *transcendent* to the weak human person, which is imposed on him so that he can surpass himself and encounter others as he renders them their due. The modern world superbly ignores the fact that society is founded on the very nature of things, that it is not a creation of man's free will. It fails to understand the family and ties of blood which naturally predispose man to unity. It forgets that custom and historical coexistence are second nature. It refuses to adopt the extraordinary expression of Rivarol, which encapsulates the relationship between the social and the sacred: "Every state is a mysterious ship which is anchored in heaven."[5] The modern world celebrates "the eminent dignity of the human person," who is

---

[5] Antoine de Rivarol (1753–1801), French royalist journalist and translator. The citation is from his *Discours sur l'homme intellectuel et moral* (1797).

essentially *incommunicable*. How could this world then be endowed once more with a real society, a true *common* good, and authentic general justice, the protector and guarantor of particular justice? How to once again pass from the *incommunicable to the communicable* without a violent show of force which crushes and fuses the so-called citizens into an amorphous, anonymous mass?

XI
CONDITIONS FOR UNITY

NO ONE DOUBTS THAT IT would be difficult to attain union of minds and hearts. Yet this is not impossible, as demonstrated by the Egyptian empire, ancient city-states, Rome, and medieval monarchies and republics. These societies lasted as long as they preserved the same conception of man, the world, and God, in its broad outlines in conformity with reality. Without these concepts, the common good would never have existed. The common good and common sense, a natural form of intelligence and the receptacle of earthly and heavenly eternal truths, are inseparable from each other.

But this necessary condition is not sufficient. For man to heed the demands of general justice, which orders his acts to the common good, it is also necessary that a certain common morality hold sway in the social sphere where he conducts his activities. How could one be a good citizen when he hands himself over to intemperance, to just the pursuit of pleasure, always implacably self-referential, or if, on the contrary, deprived of sensitivity, affection, and desires he becomes mired in a form of puritanism, which in turn is just as unfailingly selfish? Or how could one be a good citizen when he either fears nothing or fears everything and yields to violence or pusillanimity? Both the irascible and the fearful persons are equally riveted to their own egos, one a mighty brute and the other a cowardly beast. How, in the end, could one be a good citizen if he does not practice the virtue of prudence, which applies general principles of conduct to specific situations and endows all human acts with reason, relevance, and order? A man deprived of reason, hasty, rash, unthinking, incapable of choosing the means appropriate to the ends he is striving for, is a disturber of the public order and the common good. The exercise of the virtue of general justice presupposes the exercise of all the other intellectual and moral virtues, which it brings to their point of perfection.

Thus, justice is not seated in the intellect, taken as the faculty of knowledge: we are not called just from the fact that we know something with accuracy, but from the fact that we accomplish something with rectitude. Justice is then necessarily seated in the appetitive faculty. But "there are two kinds of appetite, that is, the will which is in the reason (*voluntas quae est in ratione*), and the sentient appetite which follows upon the perception of the senses ... But to give each his due cannot depend on the sentient appetite because perception of the senses does not go so far as considering the relation of one thing to another; this is proper to reason. Therefore, justice cannot have the irascible or concupiscible appetites

as its subject, but is seated only in the will. This is
why the Philosopher defines justice as an act of the
will."[1] Now since the will can only will the universal good, the common good, and since it infuses its
energy into the acts of the other virtues, regardless of
their respective objects, it follows that general justice
so to speak channels towards itself the whole of the
virtuous life, and that it is the virtue par excellence
to which are subordinated prudence, fortitude, and
temperance, along with virtues related to them.

Aristotle compares justice to the evening star and
the morning star, to the *stella rectrix*[2] that infallibly
directs the sailor through the immensity of the sea
towards the port.[3] It is not at all surprising, then, that
St. Thomas holds the practice of natural religion to
be the first of the virtues derived from general justice
which encompasses it and directs it: the will, the
rational appetite, the love of the universal good and
the common good at least implicitly, for general justice, consist in the love of the universal Good and the
ultimate End of all human acts, whom we call God.

The relationship of general justice to general morality is like that of the base of a cone to its vertex. In the
least important virtues, there is revealed a hidden consideration for others: the chaste man never commits
adultery. Whoever controls his passions truly serves
the common good by providing his will with a way

---

[1] *Summa Theologiae*, II-II, q. 58, art. 4, c. The reference to
Aristotle is from *Nicomachean Ethics*, V, 5.
[2] Lodestar.
[3] *Nichomachean Ethics*, V, 1.

out which does not prejudice his own end. Conversely, ages in which passions are given free rein are those in which society is undermined. When Eros is no longer restrained, the times are ripe for revolution. Licentiousness and the mania for constructing artificial uninhabitable "societies" with a great deal of ink and drivel, which ran rampant in the eighteenth century, contributed more to the overthrow of the Ancien Régime than all the political failings of the French monarchy: they dismantled the keystone of the social edifice which always depends on good morals and the certitude provided by common sense. An aphrodisiac civilization enslaves man to the incommunicable pleasures of the flesh and immures him in an egocentricity with no door or window open to the outside world. The intellect then breaks off access to the paths which connect it to reality and feeds on its own wild imaginings. The rational animal changes into a convoluted pleasure-seeking highbrow. The social animal who is one and the same with him is transformed into an enemy of man whose exclusive devotion to himself is crowned with a garrulous love for an ideal humanity which exists only in his mind and becomes confused with himself. Society collapses. Montaigne observed that "supercelestial opinions" are in happy harmony with "subterranean morals,"[4] but he had not foreseen the consequences: the sacrifice of millions of human beings of flesh and blood to the idol of the State in the Sky. Our century has not yet seen the end of this.

---

[4] *Essais*, 1580.

XII
THE CONSEQUENCES
OF THE REJECTION
OF THESE CONDITIONS

WHAT DO OUR CON-temporaries actually have left when they have renounced the primacy of the speculative intellect which unites them in a commonly-held affirmation of fundamental realities, and when they have lost those virtuous *habitus*, "not easily displaced" as the scholastics say, which orient them towards one and the same common good under the irresistible impulse of the practical intellect? Nothing, if not the "poetic" intellect, the intellect at work, transforming the external world, producing material goods, creating a "new man" and a "new society": the unprecedented diminution of contemplation and the great decline of morals in the modern age are closely correlated to the prodigious conquests of technology. Since the Renaissance, *knowing* for the sake of knowing and *acting* as an upright man, in the fully moral sense that this adjective still had in the seventeenth century, have given way to *doing*. The world has become an enormous construction site and society, a massive factory. Humanity is going backwards, as it glorifies itself, towards an ant colony, the perfect form of animal societies.

This spectacle is fascinating. There is no longer a speculative intellect, and its object, a common world, has vanished into thin air. There is no longer a practical intellect: the ensemble of ends common to every civilized man has become undone and each of them has been destroyed. There remain only idiosyncratic worlds, only open to subjective feelings, worlds implacably private which do not communicate among themselves. The modern man lives, so to speak, in a world without ontological depth, in which being and essence are no longer imposed on intellects formerly in accord with them, and in which ends no longer present themselves compellingly to the will. Living in a world which is their own, not shared with anyone, man is at the same time situated in a world in which are excluded truth, the ground of agreement among all minds, and the good, point of convergence for all those with a rational appetite.[1] What then is a world with neither truth nor goodness, save *a world without being, without reality*, since the true is being as comprehended by the intellect, and the good is being as an object of the will. The modern world is *a world of appearances*, which never *exists* and which is ceaselessly *becoming*, a world of processes and metamorphoses, a world which is continually evolving, a world in flux, a world in a permanent state of revolution.

[1] i.e., a will.

In this world which is continually capitulating in the face of flights of fancy and desire, how can we introduce even a temporary element of stability without which it would be truly unlivable, unless by conferring from without on its amorphous, malleable substance forms borne of human industry and specifications coming from the will of man?

In other words, *the modern world can now only be something to fashion, to shape, to transform*. It can now only be *an object on which are exercised the creative intelligence of man and his will for* power. The modern world is the creation of man. It is the world of Technology, the world of Work, the world of Means for man to transform the world. That is to say, modern man deprived of his natural speculative and moral activities, finds himself in the presence of a world in which he can only carry out his transitive function, through which, like an artist, artisan, or worker, he stamps external matter with the projects of his intellect and the designs of his will. In other words, then, man cut off from his relation to a common world and the ends common to his nature, confronted with a world with which he no longer communicates naturally, *reduced to his pure subjectivity, to his solitary ego, has no other resource, since he is unable to live without a world around him, than to construct a new, artificial world together with other subjectivities, thereby establishing agreement among those with free-ranging thoughts and autonomous wills.*

XIII
THE DISAPPEARANCE
OF JUSTICE

THE QUESTION IS TO KNOW if such an endeavor is condemned to fail from the start because its principle is a *radical lack of realism*. It is important to reiterate as an urgent matter, as required by the urgent situation, that this originates from the negation of the primacy of the speculative intellect in the order of contemplation and from the concurrent rejection of the sovereignty of practical reason in the order of action, along with consigning being and the good, as respectively defined by these faculties, to oblivion.

The characteristic feature of individual subjectivities in their nakedness, dispossessed of any differences among them having to do with being and the good, which make distinctions among them, is to be entirely similar. An intellect deprived of its conformity to an object which defines it is equal to another in the same situation. An empty thimble is like an empty barrel. Thus, "societies" constructed by man in modern times have nothing of the social: as we have already said, they are *dis-societies* formed by identical atoms who no longer offer each other mutual assistance because they have nothing to give each other, and who thus have no reason to be united. The notion of the common good or the public interest, formerly quite vigorous even at the time of great social calamities, is obliterated in the face of individual interests and special interest groups, the latter forming a coalition with individual interests. Contemporary "societies" now only *appear* to be societies, and general justice — or what is termed social justice, ironically no doubt — the development of which they claim to promote, is only a bogus concept taken over by egotists who have banded together. We shall see later that two specific forms of justice, distributive and commutative, do not fare any better. The prodigious use of the words "justice" and "injustice" employed by everyone, and which no one on earth over the past two or three centuries has tired of, is the unequivocal sign of this curious state of affairs. The diagnostic of Maurras is incredibly perceptive: "There was an Ancien Régime; there is not yet a new regime; there is only a state of mind tending to prevent this regime from coming to birth."[1]

Let us get to the heart of the matter: the essence of every society is *to bring together unequal individuals* in view of common ends, an indispensable condition for a better life. This is witnessed by the most basic of human societies, based on the difference between the sexes and destined for the purpose of propagating

---

[1] *La Politique naturelle*, 1937.

life. As Henry Allen Moe, president of the American Philosophical Society, stated in 1965, regarding the expression of Thomas Jefferson which inspired the Declaration of Independence in Philadelphia in 1776 and the famous Bill of Rights in 1789, "all men are created equal": "I dare to say flatly now that few unqualified statements have done more harm than this.... To say that all men are created equal is, as everybody knows and nobody doubts but nobody says, the apotheosis of error." The corollary immediately follows: society precedes the individuals which form it and whom it organizes into a hierarchy; therefore, the construction of *a new society*, the result of the free decision of its future members, held to be equal, belongs to the mythology of our times. The project is unfeasible.

XIV
DEMOCRACY, FRUIT OF A DIS-SOCIETY

THERE IS A BIG DIFFERENCE, however, between knowing and being persuaded! Every society, healthy or ailing, united or torn apart, produces political institutions in conformity with its condition. Modern dis-society has engendered modern democracy. It is hardly necessary to recall here that this system is not at all comparable to ancient and medieval democracies, which presupposed solid social bases connected among themselves, which *by their nature* did not call into question the prior existence of the society and the common good, more important than the wills of individuals. Modern democracy shares the unreal character of modern "society." It is part of its very essence to exist only via words. The egalitarian principle on which it is established vanishes as soon as it goes into operation. Neither just before nor just after the establishment of the rite of universal suffrage in which all participate on equal terms, does democracy exist: as in nature, the hierarchy, pushed out the door, comes back in through the window. There is no equality between those who

possess the financial and material means to disseminate propaganda and those who are subjected to it,
voluntarily or not. There is no equality between the
people and their representatives and ministers. There
is no equality between the majority and the minority.
Democracy is in reality an "aristocracy" in disguise.
As soon as it is established, it disappears and changes
into its opposite. Under the alleged reign of Numbers
and the Masses there is concealed the power of an
oligarchy to which in varying degrees are joined the
power of Money and the power of Sophistry, which
both have the goal of making hoodwinked citizens
take a sow's ear for a silk purse. Behind this regime
similar to that of the Merovingian kings, one must
look for the mayors of the palace.[1] Regurgitating the
same old egalitarian words permits some to become
the equals of their superiors and the superiors of their
equals. As George Orwell writes in his novel *Animal
Farm* regarding citizens indoctrinated and dazed by
the egalitarian myth, "All animals are equal, but some
are more equal than others."

On the other hand, in a society where the primacy
of the speculative intellect is only exercised under the
rudimentary form of the common sense of the people
and where the correlative influence of the practical
intellect only influences behavior under the ordinary form of good morals, public opinion no longer
exists. As it is impossible to live with one another

---

[1] Under the Merovingian dynasty (mid-fifth to mid-seventh
centuries) the mayors of the palace over time came to wield the
real and effective power in the kingdom.

without a minimum of cohesion among minds, the
disappearance of a way of thinking, more or less
reasonable, more or less correct, implicitly referring
to a system of immutable truths, has been compen-
sated by the appearance of another type of public
opinion, contrived, responding to the imperative of
the poetic intellect whose authority prevails. Then
public opinion, confronted with an amorphous mass
of unfounded subjective judgments, supplies the
intellect with a form and an object, produced on an
industrial scale in thought factories which serve to
call forth human actions and which proliferate today
under the social rubric of "Information." The actual
state, custodian of the national will, and the legal
state which is the expression of this will, find themselves dispossessed of their power to the benefit of an
intelligentia, itself in the service of the most diverse
special interest groups — parties, trade unions, and
more or less covert organizations — which contend
among themselves, band together, part ways, team
up in other groupings, and behind the scenes agitate
in order to take charge of the state. The dis-society
under their power is doomed to perpetual fluctua-
tion, until a more powerful collaborator eliminates
all the others. For the citizen that could be taxed
and subjected to unpaid labor at the hands of the
Ancien Régime is substituted the tractable, easily
manipulated citizen of a system yet to be named, in
which nature, outraged, artificially reconstitutes the
hierarchies which egalitarianism has amputated from
it. A widespread malaise ranging from agitation to

torpor, caused by endless manipulation of the human mind, replaces the common good and reconstitutes a kind of degraded general justice, the result of a sort of universal societal neurosis.

Obedience to the demands of general justice and the subordination of the part to the whole are, in effect, so deeply rooted in human nature that, in its horror of the void, it immediately fills it with a replacement product whose effectiveness has been shown to be, up to the present, infallible: Democracy, capitalized, deified, erected as the absolute, indisputable principle of the "social order." In the eyes of its numerous devotees, fueled by enthusiasm or passively enmeshed in the gears of its political liturgies by those who "pull the strings" in the system, casting doubt on the excellence of democracy and even more on its existence constitutes a type of inexpiable crime against humanity.[2] To call democracy into question is an attack on the dignity of the human person, a mortal wound inflicted on each ego.

We have demonstrated above that society precedes and is superior to the individuals who form it and that the common good which unites its members is for them "something divine" and transcendent. There is no society without a bond to the transcendent or without religion. "Democratic society" does not escape from this law. Professor Georges Burdeau, who holds the chair of constitutional law at the Faculty of Law of Paris, declares without hesitation in the

[2] *Lèse-humanité* in French.

first sentence of his book on the subject: "Democracy today is a philosophy, a way of life, *a religion and, almost incidentally, a form of government.*"[3] *A religion of Liberty*, in the singular like God, and more precisely, *a religion of the Liberation of man* has been substituted for the classical mode of democracy centered on the defense and exemplification of specified limited human liberties. This happened in the measure to which the Christian religion, transcending natural religion in the West, lost its authority. Democracy is a prolongation of the Christian religion, which it eliminates and replaces. It brings man the promise of freedom from evil, but in democracy evil is found in the social organization that subjects man to laws which are not proper to him, but rather the expression of his total autonomy. It calls into question any social order constructed of any kind of obligation or constraint. It is the projection, in the horizontal dimension of time, of the vertical dimension of eternal salvation which Christ promises to those who follow Him.

The entire destiny of each individual is thus implicated in the implementation of democracy: each person can only be fully human insofar as democracy frees him from all subordination to what is not himself. This is why winning political rights is only secondarily the goal of democracy. We can observe in the middle of the twentieth century numerous countries in which inhabitants are deprived of civil liberties and which

[3] *La démocratie*, 1969. Emphasis is De Corte's.

are no less openly classified as democratic. The goal of democracy is the construction of a new "society" in which each individual enjoys the most complete freedom, whose conduct is under no obligation or sanction, and whose ego is his own absolute. Democracy is thus always under construction. There must always be more democracy. It is not enough for the system to guarantee rights. Through a permanent denial of all natural, semi-natural, and organizational bonds that unite the individual to others, it must create out of nothing a "new world," co-extensive with the planet, in which each person relies only on the dictates of his autonomous conscience. As long as there are still people in the world who are subject to others in some way, there could not be a true democracy, since there would be no possibility for each individual to fulfill his potential in complete equality with everyone else. Democracy is the modern form of a crusade.

It is also the modern form of ecumenism. A democracy which would not be universal is inconceivable, since that would be a self-contradiction. The destiny of one individual can only be fulfilled if all people fulfill theirs. Living in society is a necessity. The human person is not walled up within his own egotism. He is dependent on a community. The development of the person and the common good go hand in hand, and the fulfillment of the individual coincides with that of humanity united at last under a world government which will ensure the redemption of all people, the suppression of all forms of slavery, and universal beatitude.

We are not exaggerating. Woodrow Wilson articu-
lated the charter of this apostolic, triumphal democracy: *to make the world safe for democracy*;[4] this
philosophy inspires our age. The rush of events which
since May 1968[5] have transformed the mentality of
lay and ecclesiastical clerics make sufficiently clear to
us that the contemporary *intelligentsia* sees itself as
committed to the mission of spreading the good news
of the complete liberation of man and of breaking
down the last barriers maintained by weak govern-
ments and tottering religious hierarchies.

---

[4] Italicized phrase is in English in the original; Wilson invoked
this justification for leading the US into World War I. [De Corte's
attribution of the quote to Roosevelt has been corrected.]
[5] Referring to a period of civil unrest in France, with the occu-
pation of universities, demonstrations, and a general strike, a
reaction against capitalism and US imperialism.

X V
DEMOCRACY AS A
DESECRATED CHURCH

EMOCRACY THUS reverses the relationship of the elements of society. While for traditional philosophy and in the customs of civilized peoples, the parts are subordinated to the whole, it is now the whole which is subordinated to its parts. Democratic "society" in gestation has the goal of giving birth to a new Absolute: the deified human person, the man whose existence, always concrete and unique, is identified with his universal essence. Rousseau, occasionally lucid in the midst of his fantasies, had already understood this: for him, democracy is made for "a nation of gods."[1] Democracy is precisely the desecration of the Catholic Church, its transposition and realignment to the horizontal axis of temporal happiness, the earthly reconstruction of paradise lost, the proclamation of the redemption of each individual, who, believing in democracy, is baptized in its "spirit" and "truth." It inverts the relationship between

[1] *Du contrat social*, 1762.

grace and nature: the supernatural becomes natural and thus destroys itself and nature along with it. Christ distinguishes between God and Caesar, between the Church as a supernatural society and the natural society of the polity, according to the vertical dimension where, far from opposing each other, they arrive at a compromise, thus clearly noting the distinction and complementarity of these orders, correlative and not opposed to each other. But democracy politicizes, collectivizes, and secularizes the Christian religion, which then becomes an instrument of its realization, as the Christian religion is converted into a democracy in which the cult of Man eliminates the cult of the Divinity.

The message of democracy is similar to the Gospel, which does not proclaim salvation for human societies and civilizations, but is addressed only souls, which are irreducibly personal. Whereas the Gospel reveals the mystery of the next life, where there will be neither husband nor wife, Greek nor gentile, where the resurrected will have no other bond among themselves than God Himself, their supernatural common good, democracy, which reduces the content of the common good to the here and now, and appeals to individuals uprooted from communities of their birth to which they are destined and who are now given over to consumerism or subversiveness. Democracy sets itself up as a "mystical body" whose cohesiveness it claims to guarantee through the mere power of its ideal. Democracy carries out in time the role which the supernatural common good fulfills in eternity, the latter alone capable of uniting persons whom death has taken away from their earthly cities since it transcends the forces of nature. Democracy, then, appropriates the place of the God of Christian revelation. In spite of the radical secularism to which this usurpation condemns it, Bergson goes as far as to say that democracy is evangelical in essence.[2] Nothing could be truer, provided that we note that democracy and the Christian faith are like two geometric figures which when superimposed can only perfectly match up when one of them adjusts itself to the other, completely rotating on its axis. Democracy is at once the counterfeit and the antithesis of Christianity. It is not surprising to observe that everywhere democracy becomes established it drives out its model. Here we see the application of Gresham's law, which holds that bad money drives out good. Christian democracy is a contradiction in terms: the noun automatically eliminates the adjective. Look on the one hand at the PSU[3] and the CFTD,[4] and, on the other at Chili[5] and Italy,[6] as well as the "democratization" of the Church since Vatican II.

[2] *Les deux sources de la morale et de la religion*, 1932. Henri Bergson (1859–1941) was a French philosopher.
[3] *Parti socialist unifié*, the Unified Socialist Party, whose ideology ranges from Christian socialism to an alternative communism.
[4] *Conféderation française du travail*, French Democratic Confederation of Labor, established in 1919 as an organization of Christian workers, but secularized in 1964.
[5] Possibly referring to *Cristianos por el socialismo*, Christians for Socialism, active from 1971 to 1973.
[6] Perhaps a reference to the *Partito Cristiano Sociale*, the Christian Socialist Party, active between 1944 and 1948.

It causes no further surprise to see democracy proclaim its identification with justice. Just as justice according to the Gospel is a general term encompassing all conduct in conformity with the will of God, democratic justice is the alignment of all people with the principle of equality and liberation with regard to everything that affects the autonomy of the human person. Justification according to St. Paul is based on the conversion of man who from then on no longer belongs to himself, but to Jesus Christ and His work of redemption. Similarly, and as it characteristically changes the pro into a contra, democracy renders just all acts which free man from social constraints, from all allegiance to another, and ultimately, from everything, to restore man to himself in sole ownership and complete sovereignty. Christianity provides man with the end of objective beatitude: God. Democracy calls man to the realization of his complete subjectivity. For there to be justice according to democracy, it is necessary and sufficient for each man to be a person and treated as such, in other words for him to rely only on his own will, regardless of any connection he might have with objective ends which are independent of the will and which would be determinative for it.

XVI
THE STATE WITHOUT SOCIETY

HIS IS THE REASON WHY throughout the world, to a greater or lesser extent depending on the social reserves which each people has been able to retain and which have not yet been totally exhausted by the system, we find ourselves in the presence of a *state without society*, of a *state towering over a dis-society*. There is not and cannot exist in democracy an *unbiased* environment suited to the exercise of the virtue of general justice, nor a *real* common good to orient this virtue, nor any union, consensus, or *effective* partnership among all citizens, imposed by the nature of things. Democracy is an *idea*, a *figment of the imagination*, whose distinctive characteristic is to exist, as a *subjective* representation, only in the mind that conceives it. It is a kind of ideological plasma in which individuals bathe, a myth which enmeshes each person in a secret cult, professed by each, of his own *ego*. The common good in a democracy, if one can still refer to it as such, can only be the democracy itself, which only unites people in the imagination. To keep them effectively united, in spite of the dis-society where they are located, there only remain the machinery of the state and the police apparatus. In every democracy, state control and law-enforcement systems *must* be on the increase.

Nevertheless, it is not enough to say this. This state without a society, without a true common good, in which general justice has no political role, leaves no place for distributive justice, an extension of general justice.[1] Only commutative justice remains, which governs interpersonal transactions. This is the only form of justice still functioning in contemporary dis-societies, along with remnants of general and distributive justice characteristic of the natural and semi-natural communities which still subsist after a fashion and which are tending to die out. Yet if commutative justice still survives, it is by undergoing a profound transformation. In fact, commutative justice, part of particular justice,[2] as its name indicates deals with transactions among persons and exclusively involves specific goods which individuals give to each other as part of an exchange. What it regulates does not come only from the equivalency which it establishes between what is borrowed and repaid, so that the person who possesses something belonging to another must return to him exactly what is owed him, even if the debtor ends up with a greater quantity of

[1] However, general justice is seen as a separate category from distributive justice by most authorities. General justice concerns the duties of individuals toward the community, while distributive justice governs the duties of the government toward the members of the community.
[2] Particular justice has two forms, distributive justice and commutative justice.

the object of the transaction. In this case, if there is question about the amount to be returned, it is determined according to an arithmetical average.[3] An additional factor here is the influence of general justice on particular justice as on all the virtues in the context of the harmony that reigns over the entire community through its agency. Particular goods can only be exchanged among persons in an orderly, conflict-free manner if general justice, responsible for the common good, applies to their transactions in a kind of redundancy.[4] The private domain is only preserved from disorder if the public domain in some way imposes its preeminence and influence on it. Particular interests are only balanced out to the degree that all the members of the community implicitly or explicitly pursue the public interest and are united among themselves. In this case, the state, guardian of the public interest, only deals with individuals to sanction offenses that they could always commit. The private domain is only exceptionally under its jurisdiction. But where the sense of the common good diminishes, where the public interest gives way to special interest groups and coalitions among these under the influence of an egalitarian, divisive philosophy, the state is forced to encroach on the private domain, abandoned to the appetites of individuals and groups, unless it is itself subject to their attacks. In both scenarios, *the public domain and the private domain merge with each other.*

[3] The context and application of this passage are not clear.
[4] Since these transactions come under the jurisdiction of commutative justice, general justice does not need to be invoked. Any influence it has, then, is "redundant."

XVII
CONSEQUENCES
FOR THE ECONOMY

HE RESULT IS THAT THE economy, by its nature, origin, and purpose directed to the consumer of flesh and blood and part of the private domain for centuries, has been gravitating more and more towards the state without a society, in the grip of a process of fragmentation. The economy regulates actions of people in the production and utilization of services and material goods coming to them *essentially* because of their distinct individuality and their incarnation in a body which belongs exclusively to them and which alone is capable of producing and consuming economic goods and services.

That's not all. The nature of what is useful is to be useful to someone. To be useful to no one would be meaningless. In a closed economy of the Robinson Crusoe type,[1] a loincloth is useful to the one who makes it. In a barter economy, where the producer is different from the consumer, every object produced

---

[1] A simplified model of an economy based on one consumer, one producer, and limited goods, as is the case with Robinson Crusoe and his life on a remote island.

is destined to the consumer because it is useful both to him and to the producer, who exchanges it for another product he is in need of. This bilateral process oriented to use is facilitated in a more developed economy by the use of money. Whatever the prevailing type of economy, primitive or complex, liberal or collectivist, the movement of products in the system is always from someone to someone else, from one person to another. The economy is necessarily based on this reciprocal relationship, regulated by commutative justice.

But the state without society, a common good, or the virtue of general justice is not less of a state, the guardian of justice. It must safeguard a multitude of exchanges of specific goods and an endless stream of transactions. The state can only to this in two ways, the "laissez-faire" system, allowing free play to the relations between producer and consumer, confident that its role must be limited to ensure compliance with contracts, even if they are draconian, made between individuals or groups of individuals. Alternatively, the relationship between producer and consumer can be implemented through massive intervention, with a monopoly on production and distribution and the conviction that individuals are incapable of managing transactions among themselves. In the first case, those in partnerships with others assume the function of guardians of justice based the positions they hold, but then first some, and then others get hold of the controls of the state, which is termed *liberal*. It is the same in the second case, with this proviso, that a number of individuals or a single group has eliminated all the others and wields power in the state, which is termed *totalitarian*. History strikingly shows, moreover, that liberalism is the fundamental feature, latent as though asleep, of *sociosis*,[2] of a societal illness characterized by the disappearance of general justice, of which collectivism is the obvious feature, with its accelerated expansion. That it may be better to contract an illness under its benign, as opposed to acute, form must not make us forget the kinship between the two systems and their common origin: the state without a society.

---

[2] A neologism in both French and English meaning "social disorder."

XVIII
DEMOCRACY ENGENDERS COMMUNISM

HE STATE WITHOUT SOCI-
ety, which is the hallmark characteristic
of these contemporary times, culminates in countries where communism
has come into power, following a revolution, a social breakdown caused by war, or an
invasion. If it is true that communism, as Balzac
foresaw, is "the living and acting logic of democracy,"[1]
it cannot be otherwise. Man witnesses to his essence
even in his worst falls and his most serious aberrations: the concept he has of himself and the world,
conscious or not, guides him in all his acts. In this
respect, there is scarcely a concept of man and the
world less grounded in reality than that originating
from Marx. It has spread like a torrent through the
intelligentsia, who were uprooted from reality by
eighteenth-century rationalism, which they then
passed on to the fragmented masses, bearing them
off towards the impossible, towards nothingness.

What we have said about democracy is equally
true of communism, but it is important to repeat

[1] *Les Paysans*, 1840.

it forcefully, so incredible does it seem to assert that *communism does not exist, nor can it exist in any way*, when it has been imposed on more than a third of humanity. Socialism is a phenomenon of imaginary compensation, of mere words, which immediately arises once a society collapses and its members no longer heed the imperatives of general justice, which orders them to the common good as the greatest of their goods. Its ideology hastens the dissolution to the point of rupture of all social bonds, leading to revolution. Yet when socialism embarks on the construction of a new society conformed to its philosophy, it is obliged to give way to an oligarchic system in direct contradiction to the collectivism that inspires it. Socialism, subjected to the reality test, disappears as a reality and reverts to what it cannot not be: *a figment of the imagination*, a fantasy, a fable, a myth.

This is evident when we first read the texts of the communist bible, source of orthodoxy for the regime, and then open our eyes.

If it is true that everything is defined by its end, Marxism is neither socialist nor communist nor collectivist; it is a radical individualism, and, in technical terms, we could without the least error speak of an absolute solipsism, that is to say, according to the precise definition in Lalande's *Vocabulaire technique et critique de la philosophie*[2] the doctrine which holds that "the individual self which one is aware of, with

---

[2] André Lalande et al., *Technical and Critical Vocabulary of Philosophy*, compiled by the Société française de philosophie and published in segments in its newsletter from 1902 to 1923.

its subjective transformations, and other selves which one represents to oneself, have no more of an independent existence than dreams." We could not define theoretical and practical Marxism more accurately. Its relentless propaganda, which meets with next to no resistance, especially from the intellectuals of the mass media,[3] has given currency to a deceptive image, the most mendacious that humanity has ever known.

In fact, Marx's initial intention, which he clearly and persistently asserted and pursued to its most extreme consequences, and which has been implemented by political regimes that lay claim to his philosophy, was to liberate man from *everything* that alienates him, starting with the first, religious alienation, without which the others could not survive for long. "Religion, writes Marx, "is only the illusory sun that revolves around man *as long as man does not revolve around himself.*"[4] "Philosophy makes no secret of it. The confession of Prometheus: 'In simple words, I hate the pack of gods!' is its own confession, its own aphorism against all heavenly and earthly gods who do not acknowledge *human self-consciousness as the highest divinity.*"[5] "Religion . . . lies crushed beneath his feet, and we by his triumph are lifted level with the skies."[6] "*Man is the supreme being for*

---

[3] "Mass media" is in English in the text.
[4] *Critique of Hegel's Philosophy of Right*, 1843.
[5] Forward to doctoral dissertation, *The Difference between the Democritean and Epicurean Philosophy of Nature*, 1841.
[6] Doctoral dissertation. It is Epicurus who crushes religion, in this reference to a quote from Lucretius, an exponent of Epicurean philosophy.

man."[7] *"The root of man is man himself."*[8] Engels is the faithful interpreter of Marx when he for his part writes, "Through its essence, religion empties man and nature of their content, and transfers that content to the fantasy of a God in the next world, who, in turn, by means of grace grants men and nature a part of his superabundance."[9] "The essence that man adores and deifies as an essence foreign to him is his own essence." This is not a total repudiation of the Christian religion or other religions, but of theodicy and metaphysics. Marx and Engels, the Christ and St. Paul of atheism, categorically deny the essential and existential relationship between contingent being and the absolute Being, along with any recognition of and gratitude[10] to Him on the part of the human intellect and will. The very first step of man is to annihilate this alienation.

This psychological alienation is coupled with a physical alienation of which the social form is and can only be economic, since man, rid of God, finds himself faced with a world devoid of God, where traces of the sacred are no longer interpreted. However, the *division of labor* proper to economic activity since the origins of man has resulted in the exploitation of nature by human beings, an exploitation more and more subject to specialization and compartmentalization, and a deluge of hierarchies which organize and

---

[7] *Critique of Hegel's Philosophy of Right.*
[8] Ibid.
[9] The sources for this and the following quote from Engels have not been identified. These may not be exact citations.
[10] The text has *reconnaissance au double sens du mot.*

structure this exploitation, which is then changed into the exploitation of men by men. It is not enough to liberate the conscience; man must be emancipated from all dependence on others regarding the only life he has: his earthly existence as a worker, one who transforms the world. "A being does not regard himself as independent," writes Marx, "unless he is his own master, and *he is only his own master when he owes his existence to himself. A* man who lives by grace of another considers himself as a dependent being. But I live completely by grace of another if I owe him ... the preservation of my life."[11] The only way to eliminate economic alienation is to restore man to himself, with total autonomy, and to abolish all private ownership of the means of production by means of which those in sole possession of these means oppress those lacking them, creating inequality between them. Since people are by nature economic beings, the abolition of private ownership would make everybody equal and would being about true democracy, which is, then, according to Marx, "the essence of every political constitution."[12] In this democracy of a clearly Rousseauian cast, property becomes collectivized and all "real" human capabilities are held in common, with the desires of each citizen no longer oriented toward a particular good. He is then submerged in the common Will, and only looks to the "common good," all the while obeying only himself and remaining as free as before.

[11] *Economic and Philosophical Manuscripts*, 1844.
[12] *Critique of Hegel's Philosophy of Right.*

XIX
FROM COMMUNISM
TO "HUMANISM"

OMMUNISM, TAKEN AS collective ownership of the economy by the democratic state, *is not an end in itself for Marx: it is only an intermediate stage necessary for man whose end is himself and his radical disalienation*. Communism is, the prophet tells us, "the real moment of the emancipation and self-possession of man, the moment necessary for the evolution of history. Communism is the necessary form and energy-giving principle of the near future, yet communism as such is not the goal of human evolution."[1] The goal of history can only be the realization of its original purpose—*primum in intentione ultimum in executione*[2]—the annihilation of all forms of alienation which bind man to others, to the world, and to God, a focus on human self-awareness and work, and *the liberation of the self*. Once man has cut off the ontological bonds which connect him to the state and to others, once he can revolve around himself and take himself as the focal point of

[1] *Economic and Philosophical Manuscripts.*
[2] That which is first in intention is last in execution.

everything, his destiny is fulfilled: *he will actually have taken over his essence as his alone.*

Communism thus ends up as humanism fully lived. It puts an end to the feud "*between objectification and self-affirmation, between freedom and necessity, between the individual and the species. Communism is the riddle of history solved, and recognizes itself as the solution.*"[3] Since each ego is free, one being the equal of the other, when communism has completely mastered nature and collectivized production, when "the forces of production increase *with the development of* INDIVIDUALS *in every way* and when all the sources of collective wealth emerge," every person *taken individually* will be identical to all other persons, to all of humanity, and "society will inscribe on its banners: from each according to his ability, to each according to his needs."[4] Once everyone's material needs are assured out of the abundance born of the collective control of the production of material goods, "society" puts less and less pressure on individuals. The state will wither away.

"The reign of liberty begins only when man no longer works out of necessity and external objectives; it is then located, by nature, beyond the sphere of material production properly speaking . . . It is beyond [the necessity for work] that the development of human powers as an end in itself begins."[5] The sphere of this necessity is narrowing by the day. Engels sums up

[3] *Economic and Philosophical Manuscripts.*
[4] Marx, *Critique of the Gotha Program,* 1875.
[5] *Das Kapital,* Book III, 1894.

the whole philosophy of his master as he proclaims that by means of this philosophy "man *leaps* from the realm of necessity into the realm of freedom."[6]

We could not put it more clearly: man, whose advent is announced by Marx, is the person free from everything that is not himself, "with neither God nor master." The new "society," made up of individuals aggregated together and rooted in their subjective existence, no longer has the need to unite them in their respect for general justice and the common good, which transcend them. The goal of history is the individual rid of the last form of alienation, the social necessity of working. It is the reclamation of the self by the self and the complete realization of its absolute supremacy, when at last the ontological bonds connecting the self to others, *which are imposed on him by justice*, are severed. Marxist socialism is the negation of man defined as a social animal.

This is why communist "society" *does not exist, cannot exist, and will never exist*: a society made up of individuals who are free, equal, independent of each other, with no mutual ties, without "alienation," is nonsensical. It is absurd, contrary to reason and common sense, since it is incompatible with reality; it is unreal, imaginary, chimerical, horned and deformed.[7] It is the same with every "personalist and communitarian" society, the dream of progressive

---

[6] The "Theses on Feuerbach," 1888, written by Marx and edited by Engels.
[7] In French *cornue et biscornue*. The latter adjective is derived from words meaning "two-horned," a diabolical reference here.

Christians following Mounier.[8] When he writes that "personalism is a continuous effort to identify areas where a decisive victory over all forms of oppression and economic, social, or ideological alienation would result in true liberation for man,"[9] he is building, on paper and with words, the Marxist state in the clouds where, using the unforgettable expression from *Alice in Wonderland*, one could see "a grinning cat where there wasn't any cat." To be oriented *ad alium in communi*[10] characterizes every person really living in a real society. So-called communist society, then, gives no place to general justice, without which there is no real community and which subordinates the parts to the whole, in this way illuminating all the moral virtues of each person in a reciprocity as perfect as their union.

The so-called communist society does not exist as a society, and since one must all the same live in what can only be its counterfeit, it is only *physical* force which by way of compensation unites the alienated human atoms with one another in a compact mass. The communist myth acts as a binding agent to the degree that each individual is in the grip of the imaginary. Propaganda in Marxist countries gains control of the human mind from birth to grave to the point where it becomes intolerable. This is why Pasternak

[8] Emmanuel Mounier (1905–1950), French Catholic philosopher and theologian who espoused personalism, promoted in the journal he founded, *Esprit*.

[9] See Mounier's *Manifeste au service du personalisme*, 1936.

[10] To the other [the neighbor] in common, meaning "to the community as a whole." *Summa Theologiae*, II-II, q. 58, art.6. c.

could write that the horrific war that Germany waged against Russia brought deliverance to the Russian people: "When the war broke out, its real horrors, its real dangers, its menace of real death, were a blessing compared to *the inhuman reign of the lie*."[11]

The apocryphal society constructed by Marxism with tremendous assistance from brainwashing and rote learning is in fact a machine of unparalleled perfection which resembles a myriad of cogs made to turn in accordance with the Machiavellian logic of the government. The seat of authority is considered purely and simply as the privileged place of the will to power, which is itself embedded in a logic with an abstruse meaning camouflaging it. It is child's play to move people in no matter what direction when they are reduced to mere individuals. The *ego* severed from all relations with others, the world, and God receives support from no quarter and yields to the least pressure. A cohesive political and police apparatus is sufficient to effectively keep citizens in order, accompanied by appropriate propaganda to stir them to action. The authorities know how to exercise firm control to hold together grains of sand, naturally prone to dispersal or inertia, and to launch them in the direction they have chosen. The role of propaganda is not only to conceal the purely physical nature of the regime and the function of physical force with which the state without society is now well provided, more threatening than the forces of

[11] Boris Pasternak (1890–1960), Russian novelist and poet. The quote is from *Dr. Zhivago*, 1957.

nature. Propaganda, not about to abolish human consciousness as those judging with a narrow mind maintain, has as its goal above all to fill it with a ready-made object that it takes for reality itself, when it is emptied of its constitutive relation to reality *as a given*. The whole art of propaganda consists in taking what is imaginary for what is real, and thus transforming the illusion held as evident into the driving force of human consciousness and acts.

Nothing is easier, we repeat, when one is faced with individuals, than the annihilation of their natural and semi-natural communities, blinding them to the common good which transcends them, and always inciting them to become *other* than what they are, while breaking off, under the pretext of alienation, all congenital ties uniting them to *others*. Without a natural order, they rush towards whatever artificial order is constructed for them, like famished people rushing towards what is a substitute for food. Nature abhors a void, and, if need be, makes do with what is opposite to it, waiting for better days, except when its corrupted appetite condemns it to death. History is a mass grave of dead civilizations, dead because they have broken their ties to the natural order and have feasted on artificialities.

XX
THE COMMUNIST "RELIGION"

WHEN THE MIND IS drugged by an injection of artificial stimulants and psychic energizers with a high socialist content, the only result can be proselytism and religious fanaticism. The phenomenon of the desacralization of public life and the dethronement of the transcendent, which we have seen operating in modern democracy, are both accompanied, with heightened intensity, by the compensatory phenomena of the sacralization of the new "society" now in the making and the enthronement of the immanence proper to every chimerical illusion. The religious instinct, threatened by the negation of its object, becomes radically internalized and demands to be fulfilled. Now, as Simone Weil remarks with keen insight, the collective "is the only substitute for God,"[1] the only entity that could be identified with the *self* since it only exists in the self and by definition

[1] The French philosopher and political activist (1909–1943) actually refers to the "great beast," the mass of society, which De Corte identifies with the collective, in this citation from *La pesanteur et la grâce* (1947).

transcends individuality. It thus imitates, in consummate fashion, the nature of the divine Being which at once penetrates and surpasses all beings.

On the other hand, religion, due to its spiritual nature, is the locus of what is unverifiable. A real table is identified right away since it is a material object. Christianity is certainly not irrational and its age-old apologetic has refined to the utmost the reasons for the faithful to believe. Yet in the last analysis, the judgment made by an act of faith is not due to any of these reasons. It in no way expresses the compelling necessity of these reasons. Nor is its content provable. It comes from a free act of the will which orders it. For the intellect to submit to the object of an act of faith as it does to facts or conclusions reached by rigorous proof, it needs to wait for its encounter with God beyond death. The God of faith can only be verified in the fullest sense or known through experience in eternity. The domain of religion is the unverifiable. This is why communism is a religion, not only because it is an extension of Judaism and Christianity, heretical and devoid of the supernatural, but especially because it thus evades all manner of verification. It is not only a myth, a figment of the imagination, it is a mythology, a narrative that strives to make the myth credible, leading to an act of faith. One does not embrace communism because of rational proof or self-evident facts. An act of the will is required. Communism itself gives proof of this when it remits *to the future*, the dimension of time eminently beyond control, its own realization

and that of the new man. The "singing tomorrows,"[2]
Eden here below; Salento;[3] the Abbey of Thélème,[4]
this is not what we see today. At present we have dis-
tress, exertion, the construction of a house where no
one yet lives and where a future generation — which
one? No one knows — will one day live. When Marx
writes that "*man* (as he conceived of him, the highest
divinity) is the future of *man*,"[5] his assertion cannot
be verified because the future is unverifiable. To be
certain of this assertion, one must believe it. The
"certitudes" of Marxism are all founded on an act
of faith in the future. As we have indicated above,
man free of all his alienations is something that lies
beyond communism, which itself is for tomorrow.
The whole substance of communism pertains to the
future, the chief characteristic of which is not to exist
in the present. Communism is a religion in which
the future takes the place of eternity except for two
differences. On the one hand, the Christian faith
involves an object which is not intrinsically contradictory, while the communist faith is based on the
future realization of a man who will simultaneously
and in the same respect be an individual and a social
being, separated from *the other* by the eradication of

---

[2] *Les lendemains qui chantent* (1947), autobiography of French
communist journalist Gabriel Péri (1902–1941), shot by the Ger-
mans for his participation in the French resistance during World
War II.

[3] Region in the Italian peninsula where peace and prosperity
reign in Rousseau's novel *Émile* (1762).

[4] The utopia in Rabelais' fantasy *Gargantua* (1534).

[5] An expression widely attributed to Marx and consonant with
his philosophy.

alienations and coinciding with the entire human species; this will hold for all time since history will then have been consummated. On the other hand, the positive reasons for belief that since its birth Christianity has never ceased to invoke are solid in comparison with those advanced by communism when it displays its works. One must actually be blind not to observe that countries called communist are precisely those where communism does not exist and has never existed.

XXI
COMMUNISM DOES NOT EXIST

THIS HAS BEEN DEMON-strated and proved: we have only to refer first to their own analysts to see that the religion of socialism has penetrated the innermost machinations of the brain, and then to outside observers, to establish beyond question, evidence in hand, that communism has not yet been implemented anywhere in the least degree. The existing system in countries claiming to adhere to communism is quite simply the eternal product of every democratic regime that crosses a narrow line in the society where it is in force: the emergence of an oligarchy replacing the old aristoc-racy of prominent citizens who have vanished in the turmoil of the revolution, and, to top it off, the tyr-anny of one individual, the poisonous fruit of the *dis-society of isolated individuals*.

When general justice is no longer able to keep the parts of the whole *morally* together in the service of the same common good, with the parts of the whole organically arranged in a hierarchy, the cornerstone of the community collapses, and the edifice is rebuilt according to the unassailable laws of the merely *physical* dimension of the group *by means of material strength*. This social *physics* has nothing in common with the *nature* of a human being. It is an *artificial construct* which is not an extension of nature, *but rather vacates it and supplants it*, according to the twofold logic of the system, raw power and myth, the consequences of which then unfold. This is the distinctive characteristic of raw power, as Thucydides remarked in the famous speech which he placed on the lips of the Athenian spokesman who addressed the Melians,[1] the use of all the force at the disposal of the power. This is proper to the myth of uprooting man from the natural communities, which prevent the political power from converting into sheer physical force, similar to the mechanical forces regulating physical bodies.

Marxist philosophy, implemented by Lenin, has automatically given rise to a system which Isaac Deutscher calls substitutionism,[2] which determines the permanent structure, unchanged and unchangeable, of the regime, based on four arbitrary equivalencies, which are perfectly conformed to the scorn of Marxism for the principle of identity.[3] The first of

[1] Thucydides (c. 460–c. 400 BC), Athenian historian and general. In this speech, from his *History of the Peloponnesian War*, the Athenian conquerors of the island of Melos, off the coast of Greece, do not attempt to justify their invasion, invoking the principle that might makes right.

[2] Isaac Deutscher (1907–1967), Polish Marxist historian and political activist. Substitutionism refers to the substitution of the rule of the revolutionary party for that of the working class. See Deutscher's three-volume biography of Trotsky *The Prophet* (1954, 1959, and 1963).

[3] Every object is identified with itself.

these confuses people with the proletariat; the second,
the proletariat with the party; the third, the party
with the party apparatus; and the fourth, the party
apparatus with the head of the apparatus. Thus, the
equations "the multitude is equal to the unit" and "all
are the equivalent of one individual" are regnant, and
have never been called into question in "the greatest
political, economic and social democracy that history
has known." Trotsky noted this when he criticized
Lenin's methods of creating a state where "the party
organization would take the place of the people, the
central committee that of the party organization, and
finally the dictator that of the central committee."[4]
What is most striking is that Lenin was compelled to
have recourse to this dialectical and practical sleight
of hand because of the revolutionary situation which
he himself had created and the concept of man and
society that he got from Marx. This stratagem had
not been premeditated: it is the *necessary* consequence
of a philosophy of justice which has as its goal the
annihilation, for reasons of alienation, of all known
types of society and the rebuilding of a "new society"
starting with a *dis-society*.

It is important, then, to affirm once more that
it is not through revolutionary violence that this is
achieved. Since the social animal and the rational
animal are *convertible*,[5] one can only get to this point

[4] A loose citation from Trotsky's *Our Political Tasks* (1904).
[5] Convertible in the logical meaning of the term, that is, the two
terms "social animal" and "rational animal" can properly be used
one in place of the other. [Footnote of De Corte's.]

by paralyzing the use of man's intellect. The most tried and true method is the use of terror which benumbs reason, separates it from its natural tendency to conform itself to reality, and when it is thus emptied of content, prepares it to be filled with compensatory imagery which then frees it from the atony in which it is fixed through fear of social disaggregation. Lenin thus did not for a single moment have any doubts about the inertia of the masses. To set them in motion, the proletarian minority with the passivity corresponding to them is not enough. A more restricted minority is needed to activate this minority, incapable of "getting beyond the trade-union consciousness" according to Lenin.[6] This second minority is the party transmitting the ideology designed to restore social energies, weakened and immobilized through fear. A third minority is necessary: the party apparatus, the framework of orthodoxy which, through the steel straight jacket of the administration and police force which it creates, maintains the illusion of a "new society" which is in the process of being born and the conviction that it is important to safeguard it. Finally, the last minority is the tyrant, described by Plato[7] as the product of social disaggregation, who plays the role of the divinity in traditional societies: this is the last step in the ideology needed to build the "new society," the incarnation of the immutable social

[6] *What Is To Be Done?* (1902).
[7] In his *Republic*.

truth which no society, even an imaginary one, can dispense with. The fear of being lost in the masses like a solitary shipwrecked man in the middle of the ocean is thus exorcized.

Yet if the ideology is safeguarded, it is to the detriment of the establishment of communism itself. To preserve the ideology *and its custodians* it is necessary to build a "society" with a formidable hierarchy, the echelons of which are endowed with extensive, expanding privileges as they get closer to the top. This is in direct contradiction to the structure of communist "society," the realization of which is remitted indefinitely to the future. Far from having abolished social classes, the revolutionary violence unleashed by ideology has had the effect of reconstituting them.

XXII
THE NEW RULING CLASS

I T IS CLEAR THAT THE PHENOME-
non of the exploitation of one class by another,
which, as is known, Marxist doctrine vigorously
denounces, has incredibly intensified in the USSR.
According to the Polish economist Oskar Lange,[1]
the surplus value realized by the surplus labor that
the regime imposes on the mass of its citizens has
economic significance. Thus, in 1935 the Soviet state
purchased a hundredweight of rye from its peasants
for eight rubles and sold it to its bakeries for 93 rubles,
which got even more for it from consumers. The
same thing happened in other sectors of the economy.
Nothing has changed since then. The surplus value
always goes to the state. Now a new social class, the
apparatchiks, bureaucratic, law-enforcing, and sacer-
dotal, has gotten control of the state and, as Gilles
Martinet[2] shows in his book *Les cinq communismes*,
acts as though it were the owner of the means of production. This ownership is not legal, but it is real, if

[1] Lange (1904–1965) advocated the use of market pricing tools
in socialist economies.
[2] Martinet (1916–2006) was a French journalist and diplomat
who belong to the Communist Party from 1935 to 1937. *Les cinq
communismes* was published in 1971.

one holds to the facts and the Marxist interpretation of those very facts.

Whether we speak of Soviet Russia, Yugoslavia, China, Czechoslovakia, or Cuba,[3] the same observation must be made: "The history of the communist movement is completely dominated by the emergence of a new ruling class which should have been, *but which is not, the proletariat.*"

To be even more precise, without having recourse to Marxist terminology, which runs the risk of obfuscation in observation and analysis, we note that the phenomenon is of a rare monotony: the refusal to observe the sovereign law of unity and to serve the common good through the observance of general justice, or, when necessary, to strengthen the community and its shared future by intellectual and moral reform, gives rise to social disintegration. This leads to a decline in critical thinking in the quagmire of the ideology, which, in turn, precipitates the collapse of society. The revolution which is destructive of all natural social foundations quickly reaches its apogee, and dis-society makes way for an artificial reconstruction of life in common according to the ideological schema. This new "society," bereft of its foundation of justice, can only maintain its equilibrium due to what Nietzsche calls "the steel grip" of a state without society. This state, towering above the multitude, is colonized by a parasitical class of new rulers driven by the sheer will to power that such

[3] These are the five communist systems discussed in *Les cinq communismes.*

a state, endowed with limitless power, unfailingly
generates. A new hierarchy based on power dynamics is created. Inequities arise, which are no longer
referred by general justice to the province of mutual
assistance in the context of a shared common good.
The ideology "demonstrates" that the stratification
is only temporary; the pledge to eliminate it one
day removes it from the field of consciousness, and
the system becomes fixed in a permanent lie: a new
society is in the process of being born, when there
is only the illusion of a society.

In transposing an expression of Bergon's, one could
say that the mechanical replaces the vital in social
relations.[4] The dialectics of class struggle, far from
generating a salvific synthesis following the opposition between thesis and antithesis, has culminated
in the most permanent of prostheses, the removal
of which would result in the collapse of the system
and the return of chaos. While all human societies
develop in a consistent, steady manner, without major
setbacks if political prudence, which governs them,
unceasingly maintains harmony among members,
communist "society" is condemned to immobility.
The stranglehold of the ruling class cannot be relaxed
without questioning the existence of its members and
of the system. How could the oppression imposed
on all citizens by collective ownership of the means
of production and system-wide planning be eased

---

[4] A reference to Bergson's *élan vital*, which he saw as a creative
spiritual principle immanent in all organisms and the cause of
evolution.

without removing those in charge of each level of
the pyramidal machine? The "liberalization" of the
regime could be a temporary, well-managed ruse;
like the Hundred Flowers Campaign in China,[5] it
will never be translated into reality. "Socialism with
a human face" is an illusion.

One is thus able to discern in the Soviet Union an
essential contradiction which will lead to its down-
fall in the near future, according to Amalrik[6]: for
the regime to survive, it must change (for the characteristic feature of every regime is to change over
the course of centuries while staying faithful to the
principle inspiring it), but for the rulers to remain
in power, everything must continue to be stationary.
The permanent commitment to the regime which
the apparatchiks of popular democracies maintain in
the masses must not deceive us, for rallying them is
itself part of the art of creating an illusion of social
life where it no longer exists except as a counterfeit.
As soon as the parts of a whole violate the original
social pact and no longer render to this whole that
which is due it, as in liberal democracies, as soon as
a part of the whole replaces the whole itself and to
its own benefit works against the order required by
general justice, as in popular democracies, there is
no longer anything but the semblance of a society.

[5] A government-sponsored movement from 1956 to 1957 permit-
ting citizens to criticize the communist party. It was followed by
a brutal crackdown on critics of the regime.
[6] Andrei Amalrik (1938–1980), Soviet dissident writer. In his
book, *Will the Soviet Union Survive until 1984?* (1970) he pre-
dicted its collapse.

Whether it is a matter of the romantic, solitary "I" or "citizens" amassed in collectivities where each person sees himself multiplied and endowed with increased importance, there always occurs the revolt of the individual against the species which Auguste Comte[7] speaks of and the upsurge of private interests working against the public interest which continues today. Never has general justice, wrongly called "social justice," been so thoroughly emptied of its meaning. What is called "social justice" today is nothing other than its reverse. It is the process whereby an individual, isolated or aggregated with others, demands his due of others, instead of rendering to them what is due them. Such a demand is certainly not illegitimate, but on the condition that each individual (or at least the majority of them) plays his part and takes his place in society. We have already emphasized this: particular justice is meaningless apart from general justice, since the parts are only parts in their relation to the whole, which sets out their respective functions and proper place. Up until the eighteenth century, as Jules Monnerot[8] observes, "the concept of society in European thought is not differentiated from the concept of *society as accepted*." The acceptance of society necessarily and unquestionably implies that each person accept the place he has in society. Antiquity, the Middle Ages, and the beginning of the modern era were ages of *consent to a social existence*.

[7] French philosopher and mathematician (1798–1857) who developed the theory of positivism. See his *Système de Politique positive*, vol. IV, 1854.
[8] French sociologist (1909–1995).

XXIII
SOCIETY AND THE
COUNTERFEIT HIERARCHY

I T IS NOT ONLY DUE TO A DECREE of fate or providence that this is so; it is because there is no society without a hierarchy, and every hierarchy, with its levels, has individuals occupying the various levels. Monsieur de la Palisse could not have said it better![1] Fate and divinity are here only the expression, on a par with the absolute common good, of the necessity of a hierarchy, intrinsic to the common good of every society: without diversification among human beings, there is no community. The egalitarian mystique that has prevailed since the French Revolution in liberal regimes, if it were put into practice, would lead to a total lack of differentiation, the breakdown of the community into people in sealed-off compartments, and anarchy. The same egalitarian eschatology with its marvels inspires Marxist sermonizing, but if the "new ruling class" in communist countries shows itself through its words to be bound to this apocalypse, it ignores

[1] The French expression "verité de la Palisse" refers to a truth so obvious it hardly needs to be stated.

the facts. Liberalism and socialism seemingly thrive by caricaturing the social order that they are negating and constructing a pseudo-society in which a purely material hierarchy, founded on numbers, gold, or power, imitates the vanished hierarchies of yesteryear.

We again take up our refrain: *Reason and experience prove that the rejection of general justice and the objective common good leads to the disappearance of distributive justice,* of which the foundation, scope, and, above all, the beneficiaries are increasingly called into question. The fate of pseudo-hierarchies is that they are continually supplanted by others, as the history of the parliamentary society and of "purges" gives witness. Rivalrol[2] observed that the way glory was handed out in his time "was only a snare for virtue." What would he say today? We need not insist on this point. With regard to the justice of transactions, this is left to the law of the strongest, and the strongest are always those in charge of the machinery of the state, either directly or through intermediaries. The capitalism of money and the capitalism of people, "big business," and trade unions, are something to be rejected. The state without society, representing the public sphere, thus finds itself confronted with interpersonal transactions of which the great majority, in an age when the common good no longer has any spiritual or moral influence, are made up of economic activities geared to the production and consumption of material goods.

[2] Antoine de Rivarol (1753–1801), French writer and translator.

It does not matter whether the state is strong or weak, whether it is colonized by one or another interest group or by occasional collaboration among them, whether it is a powerful instrument in the hands of the new ruling class or of a single political party. There is no more vertical distinction between the public and private spheres, between the state and the economy. There exists a horizontal syncretism, a partial or total fusion between the two sectors of human life. We are in the presence what is most typical in contemporary history: the appearance and expansion over the entire world of states without society which absorb, in a progressive or total fashion, through cunning or force, the only societies which the revolution cannot destroy since it would then annihilate all of human life: societies made up of producers and consumers, which go from the pluralistic situation in which the private nature of their activities maintains them to the situation of national, transnational, or global societies of which the state takes control.

There are always consequences, said Bainville[3]: if the state is no longer the guardian of the common good, it becomes the supplier, accountant, and manager of the specific material goods needed by each person to ensure his sustenance. It ensures its citizens, from birth to death, with the means for *life*, food, livelihood, health, physical well-being, and adds to these, as a supreme refinement, the dissemination

[3] Jacques Bainville (1879–1936), French historian and journalist with monarchist leanings.

of culture and knowledge necessary for their quasi-animal existence, including organized leisure activities, just as it delivers water and gas to residences. The state has no regard for *living better* or bridging the gap, as Plato discerns, "between the necessary and the good." Along with general justice and the particular forms of justice, concern for a *virtuous life* and a *human life,* in accord with what is most excellent in this level of life and the goals of its eminently good activities, has vanished from the modern state.

XXIV
THE "MUTATION" OF MAN

WE MUST NOT BE SUR-prised by the tolerance this modern state manifests for the most despicable pornography: since there is no longer a sphere of the private, the public sphere then being the only one accessible to man, it is, so to speak, normal for obscenity, formerly relegated to the dark backstage in the theater of the world, to flaunt itself shamelessly, with impunity, on center stage. A moral striptease becomes widespread in all sectors of human life. This exposure of the most intimate part of man's being takes every form: self-criticism and "voluntary" confessions are routine in totalitarian countries and the political mire that comes to light is not less nauseating.

The state monopoly of economic life, the end of which is always private since it is geared to the consumer in flesh and blood, who alone is able to utilize the material goods which are produced, causes a true *mutation* in the meaning of human life. Man is no longer an *intelligent* animal possessed of a *will* whose intellectual and moral activity can flourish in a political and social environment that provides for *living well* according to the intellectual and moral virtues that he possesses. He is a *working* animal whose intellect and will are put to the service of the poetic intellect, which transforms matter and makes material objects which he uses and of which he thus becomes the end. But as man is a component alongside hundreds of thousands or millions of others in the state without society, he no longer has the protections or safeguards with which natural or semi-natural communities used to liberally provide him in order to counter excesses of power. He is less and less able to take refuge and obtain help in the private sphere, which the state has increasingly taken control of.

The result is that the state controls consumption, directly or indirectly, depending on the regime, and the consumer is no longer the end of the economy. State intervention, central planning, and socialism have every-where reduced economic liberalism to a bare minimum. In countries called free, the state colonized by producers at all levels subverts the purpose of the economy and orders it solely to the benefit of producers or the few who are in charge. This is the case in totalitarian coun-tries where state power, with the proletariat as dictator in name only and the members of the state machinery as the real autocrats, constitutes the end of all work-related activity. The state becomes a gigantic factory whose only function is to continually increase the gross domestic product. It is a state made up of workers, a state whose only driving force is work, a state which, under the guise of glorifying work, has no other end other than expanding without limit and ensuring that the person located at the top has unrestricted power.

XXV

ONE INDIVIDUAL,
A SUBSTITUTE FOR UNITY

THIS ASYMPTOTIC POINT[1] IS never reached, even in the Stalinist concept of the state. Yet it belongs to the logic of the system. An industrial state, a state where politics is identified with the economy, can never avoid being centralist, with all the power at the disposal of one ego. The expression of Goethe is definitive here: "one brain is enough for a thousand arms."[2] To effectively coordinate all sectors of economic activity, the "team" and "collegial" power are not enough, for the workings of the system are not automatically coordinated among themselves: the synthesizing can only be effected in the brain of one person. As Simone Weil says somewhere, "one" in one mind and "one" in another can never make "two."[3] Only one mind is capable of gathering together all the facts concerning a problem. Recent history admirably shows that this is

[1] In geometry, an asymptote on a graph is a straight line which constantly approaches a given curve without ever meeting it. Thus, an asymptotic point refers to a given value or condition which is approached but never attained.

[2] *Faust.*

[3] See Weil's "Réflexions sur les causes de la liberté et de l'oppression sociale" (1934) in *Oppression et liberté* (1955).

indeed the case. When the last world war transformed states into gigantic arms industries involving all citizens in various capacities, each state was crowned with the power of one individual, in democracies as well as in other regimes. This is sufficiently proved by the "prestigious" names given to city streets throughout the world: Roosevelt, Stalin, and Churchill, not to mention De Gaulle, or, as an example of preterition,[4] Hitler and Mussolini, supposing their factories had been able to eliminate the massive competition from the other states.

We continually find the first social law, which prevails over all the others and which our unseeing age no longer perceives: when people no longer live together *for the sake of* each other out of obedience to general justice, inscribed in their nature and engraved in their conduct by sound institutions, they can only project their feeble individualities, side by side, puffed up by ideology, onto one unique individual *who represents them and in whom they recognize themselves in their own aggrandized divine image*, thus recovering in the Unique Individual their lost unity. The "personality cult" is inherent in the anonymous industrial state which functions like a modern army whose members are subject to one sole commander, and the "personage" who rises to the top is its answer to the "titans of Industry," which the nineteenth-century economy, bereft of a purpose, spread throughout the earth.

This is why, since Napoleon, in his own words, tried to "banish" the effects of the Revolution which

---

[4] The rhetorical technique of mentioning something briefly to highlight its importance.

overthrew the Ancien Régime without replacing it, modern industrial states are similarly military states with an imperialist vocation. They cannot function without going beyond their borders since their only objective is constant expansion. Social "egotism," which with the disappearance of general justice immobilizes their citizens, ripples over into national "egotism" and one *Ego*, which becomes one with social egotism. This process undoubtedly does not proceed at the same pace everywhere, and, by definition, cannot, since it proceeds by means of conquering. But Pan-Germanism, Pan-Slavism, Pan-Americanism, Pan-Arabism, Pan-Africanism, and so many other forms of imperialism, openly acknowledged or dissimulated, temporarily successful or aborted, successful for a time or under development, are examples of the pattern we have just identified, at once economic and tactical. It is characteristic of a kind of cone, the base of which widens under pressure of an internal necessity until it meets with an insurmountable obstacle from a similar cone. The entire history of the last two centuries is condensed here. It follows an inexorable logic.

To follow this process, we have to dispel the ideological fog surrounding it which hides its inner workings, always the same, which the system engenders out of internal necessity, as infallibly as the force which governs the fall of objects: as soon as one leaves the properly *human* social sphere, subject to the requirements of general justice, one enters, in spite of any reluctance, all at once or in spurts, the domain of physical determinism where there is no longer either good or liberty.

XXVI
A NEW IDOL: WORK

HE REFUSAL TO ACCEPT THE "invincible primacy of the true and the good" drives modern man not only to subjectivism with all its individualist, liberal, libertarian, collectivist and communist consequences, ever prey to the rifts, divisions, and conflicts that these doctrines tirelessly create; he also finds himself, like Robinson without Friday, in the presence of a world whose depths he no longer understands. As a result, the ultimate objective of this world, and, consequently, all intermediate objectives, have become opaque to him. The Christian distinction between the interior and exterior worlds has in some way become sclerotic. With its symbols redirected from their meaning and envisioned in a mathematical sense instead of being thought out and experienced, man's *ego* no longer faces a world which he can love and understand as a path leading step by step to God, but a kind of chaos, a jumbled confusion, an unintelligible entity onto which he can only project *his own bodily needs*. These are ordered so that this entity can be subjected to his intellect and will, eager to reclaim their object. For modern man the world is then no longer an ensemble of realities to which his intellect, eager for the truth, and his will, oriented to the good, must submit, but a sort of plastic material, external to himself, amorphous regarding the needs he wants to satisfy, possessed of limitations he must overcome, and onto which he puts his prevailing predatory seal, to *make* of it something useful to himself. It is evident that man thinks of himself as a kind of *artifex*[1] who *works on* the world like the worker who shapes parts of this world to make of them *manufactured objects* which *depend on* him and of which he *constitutes the end*.

This process, this action by which man changes the world through his work, has no end. Man is the goal, it is all too clear, for the useful is advantageous to him alone. However, objects produced by human artifice become, directly or indirectly, *instruments*, manufactured objects, which *serve him* to carry out other operations to control and conquer the world, other labor-intensive activities by which he establishes himself as *owner* of the world with the result that *work*, which encapsulates those activities, is from this perspective *the essential characteristic of man*. His intellect is the *means* by which he brings to the world the understanding he has of his needs. His will is the *means* by which he exercises his power on the world to satisfy them. *His work is never finished*, for the objects of his intellect and will have an infinite range. His intellect encompasses *everything* that exists, his will desires *everything* that is good, and, riveted to the single axis

---

[1] Artisan or maker.

of poetic activity, they retain these characteristics: the intellect has the task of *endlessly* producing *new* manufactured objects, and the will that of *tirelessly* using them to strengthen its hold on the world. The *totality* of existence and of the good is thus transformed into an interminable *production*, always taken up anew, the result of the labor-intensive activity of man. Man is the cause and the end of this production.

Because man has put under interdict his two properly *human* functions, contemplative activity, the province of his intellect, and practical or moral activity, the domain of his will, man is dialectically driven to become the demiurge of the world, not in order to contemplate it and love it in the splendor of its perfection, as in the fable of *Timaeus*,[2] but to endlessly transform it, and, since his needs are constantly recreated in step with these metamorphoses, to be endlessly transformed in turn. Marx provided the charter for this new *humanism of work*: "Man is the future of man": through work understood in its metaphysical radicalism, man becomes, according to a further prophecy of Marx "the highest divinity." He is a god who *creates* himself, a god in the process of becoming.

Counter to all past civilizations, the most primitive as well as the most advanced, and especially in contrast with the one born at Athens, Jerusalem, and the two Romes, the modern age is placed under the banner of *action*, understood not in the former sense of properly human activity issuing from practical reason,

---

[2] A dialogue of Plato's in which the creation of the universe in its ordered beauty is described.

from the willing intellect or the intelligent will, the object of which is the good, but as an operation producing an external effect, undertaken to shape matter in the sphere external to the agent, who exercises on it a transformative pressure, enabling it to satisfy his own needs. His banner is inscribed with Faust's words, "In the beginning was the deed," *Am Anfang war die Tat*, the opposite of the prologue of the Gospel of St. John, "In the beginning was the *Logos*": the Intellect, the Word. The counterpart of this is *Am Anfang war die Kraft*, "in the beginning was Power," the power of man as creator who supplants all transcendent creative causes. This is, so to speak, normal: must not the new god be more powerful than the One he banishes from the world scene?

Work then becomes the premier virtue of man, more precisely the only virtue, the one which replaces all the others, rendering them useless. Work is no longer experienced as a physical necessity imposed on man by the inexorable cycle: work to live, live to work, as an animal seeks its sustenance which allows it to live in order to seek it again. It is the human characteristic par excellence, by force of which man strives for the good, the only true good: the fulfillment of his being. It is the very essence of man which is realized. The fabulist himself falls prey to this:

> Work hard, spare no toil,
> Labor brings the truest gain. [3]

---

[3] "The Laboring Man and His Children," a fable of Jean de la Fontaine (1621–1695) extolling the ethic of hard work.

The classes that work, first the bourgeoisie, then the proletariat, are the superior classes, if not in fact, at least in dignity. A word derived from *tripalium*,[4] an instrument of torture, and experienced as a punishment in the past, work is now the ultimate goal which man must attain if he wants to be a man. "If you don't work, you'll never *be* anything," is the threat that all parents hold over the heads of their children in modern times. Today work has absorbed all of morality, all of politics. The only man worthy of the name is the worker. The only true state is the community of workers.

Thus, we come across the astonishing words of intellectuals who have never put shoulder to the wheel, but who have secretly aspired to be "the minds that direct a thousand hands," such as what Jean Lacroix said, taken up and theologically orchestrated, with all the wiles and sophisms of an old, seasoned Dominican, by Father Chenu[5]: "Work expresses the very substance of the human condition ... In humanizing nature, the worker becomes more of a man and in becoming more of a man, he becomes increasingly one with all of humanity and attains his objective self: the work of the proletarian humanizes the physical universe which in return universalizes him. So we have to say that it is by means of work that man is the demiurge of man." We recognize the very thesis of

---

[4] Believed to have consisted of three stakes to which those to be punished were tied and then tortured. This is the etymology of the French word for work, *travail*.

[5] Marie-Dominique Chenu, OP, influential theologian at Vatican II.

Marx, hastily whitewashed with Christianity: "Workers of the world, unite, and you will then be Catholic" or "the International[6] of workers will be the human race, and, at the same time, the new Christianity."

The attraction of this idolatry of work is such that the Catholic Church itself, in the past anchored on the knowledge and supernatural love of God, has taken to wax delirious on this and to want to beat Marxism on its own ground. According to the new theologians who inspired Vatican II, the goal is to encourage Christians brought together in a vast ecumenical movement with all the believers of other religions to create and organize, gradually or still faster through revolutionary methods, a new world where the worker can claim the title of "cooperator of God" in the work of creation. The faith moving into politics, according to the demands of the Incarnation, will thus become "credible" in the eyes of the proletariat, whom technical progress, which builds a new civilization, has made "masters and possessors of nature,"[7] apparently, and only apparently, separated from the "true God" present in their work. Let us draw out the carefully dissimulated conclusion: the clerics of all religions who have lost their positions of leadership in modern society will find them again in joining with the "new class" created by Marxism, through a process which we have described above.

[6] Communist organization of workers which existed from 1919 to 1943 and advocated world communism.
[7] From Descartes' *Discours de la méthode* (1637), referring to what man can achieve through scientific knowledge.

XXVII
WORK DETHRONES JUSTICE

IN A "SOCIETY" WHERE THE FETISH-
ism of work reigns despotically, there is no place
at all for general justice. Work is always working
for oneself (*finis cui*), to ensure one's sustenance,
to live. The person who does nothing but work, whose
horizon is limited to his work, is enclosed within his
subjectivity. A society of workers is a contradiction
in terms: it can be composed only of individuals
juxtaposed with each other. For his work to have
social value, the worker must first be integrated into
communities which share a common destiny, cause
him to escape from his subjectivity, subordinate him
to a common good, and unite him to the other members, such as the family, a business, region, or nation.
There he enters into a relationship with other parties
in a body which transcends them and gives them the
opportunity to communicate with each other, thus
constituting a true society. The worker only escapes
from his isolation when he succeeds in creating a product which he can use in an exchange with others who
are in the same situation. But that is not enough for a
society to exist, as the product involved in the transaction is immediately put to use by the individual

who needs it, by him alone. For work, the ensemble of workers, and, basically, the economy to have social significance, the economy must be integrated into an order superior to the private domain where its natural place is, and into which it is incorporated as part of its own actualization. In other words, *to live* for man, a social animal, only makes sense humanly speaking if it is directed to and in some way aspires to *living well*, to *living in accord with the good*. Then and only then do transactions between producer and consumer, governed by commutative justice, acquire social value. Economic activity, which produces useful material goods, does not have as its goal only the consumer *as such*, but the consumer *inasmuch as he is a man, a rational animal, and a social animal*. What is useful is not beneficial merely for living, but for living well, and is governed by social justice.

Here we get a glimpse of the role that general justice *should* play in contemporary "society," which is dominated by an individualist, egalitarian pseudo-democracy, a role it will never be able to fulfill as long as the man of today is incorporated into a political system for which the point of departure is everything that separates individuals and groups or puts them in opposition to each other. The inevitable endpoint of this system is the state without society, ruled by an oligarchy of parasites, yet which *could* get a fresh start, with time and propitious circumstances, beginning with the humble, inescapable realities of daily life which require unity as a prerequisite for all work in common.

XXVIII
THE ECONOMY

NDUSTRIAL "SOCIETY," WHERE labor-intensive activity reigns supreme, which we are reluctantly entering into, and which one could say is characterized by the profusion of means and the obliteration of all ends other than unlimited growth, is a "society" only in name. Due to its fixation on the particular good of individuals, the producers and consumers which constitute it, it is a *dis-society*, always vacillating between a free-for-all and forced labor, with a tendency, slow or fast according to the case, for the galleys and cudgel. Yet there is no evil without the consequences that come in its wake. The vast dominion of technology over human activities has caused the economy to go from the stage of penury or scarcity which characterized it for millenia to one of abundance and even at times overabundance. The Third World itself aspires to enter into technological "civilization": it is, as we say, "developing." The dynamism of the contemporary economy has at least the merit of freeing man from his obsession with subsistence, and ensuring that he can *live*, and be granted access to *living well*. In achieving this, there is the possibility that abundance will be jeopardized with a return to a state of scarcity. The parasitical state condemns society to this by means of economic pressure groups that siphon off for their profit the wealth created by the general economic robustness. The endpoint of this process of vampirization is already present in reality: it is the seizure of political power by a single pressure group that brings under state control, nationalizes, and organizes the dynamics of economics to its advantage. The "new ruling class," which appears on the horizon of history and leads the masses in its conquest of the state without society, is immeasurably voracious. Countries which are socialized or on the path to socialization all regress towards an economy of scarcity. To attempt to escape from this, they have no other recourse than to deploy an unbounded imperialism: these remote-controlled swarms of locusts do more damage than any kind of isolated horde of "capitalist" beasts. The colonization of the world by the state with global pretensions is underway.

To reverse this seemingly inevitable evolution, we must, somehow or other, with the means we have available, put private interests in the service of the public interest. The strength of the economy, if it is not hampered and if it does not react to this type of brake with a disordered upsurge in productive output, is our best asset. In spite of all the jeremiads about the "fallout" from technological "civilization" and its "pollution," there is scarcely anyone on the planet who repudiates its benefits and wants to go back, following the example of Gandhi, to the economy of corn

cakes and spinning wheels. Hippies do not flee to
the desert to live like hermits, but congregate in cities,
where they make use of a good many commodities. If
they travel from one continent to another, it is not on
foot. There is need for a Tartuffe to rant against the
economic "society" of our time due to its opulence
while people yield to its attractions on a daily basis:

Cover this breast which I cannot behold.[1]

A good number of "intellectuals" are guilty of
this, as they sit by the fireside in their slippers. Yet
for the person with common sense, contemporary
industrial "society" is not to be criticized because
it produces more material goods, and faster than in
the past, but because its foundations are not secure;
it requires the state, its apex, to ensure its security,
without noticing that the state transforms it into a
colony of ants. Now the dynamism which vitalizes
it is not without positive factors, of which the most
visible, yet the most unrecognized, is the *material*
solidarity established among its members. Startling
evidence of this is that they *increasingly depend on
each other*, from one end of the earth to the other,
to live and to survive. To be convinced of this, it is
enough to recall here the great crisis of 1929 and its
terrible consequences. A devaluation here leads to
another one there. The international economic system
has become a huge spider web which experiences
tremors at the least shock in no matter what place. It

[1] From Molière's play *Tartuffe* (1664), in which the eponymous
character hypocritically feigns piety and flight from temptation.

is the same in each nation and regime. Everything is connected to everything else by *material* bonds, the presence of which is felt within the daily life of men.

The dynamism of the modern economy is conditioned at every level by the division of labor that establishes among those it encompasses at each level, from a business to the whole world, a kind of community with a shared destiny, *which, though it is just material, nonetheless exists.* This phenomenon can be seen at the level of a private enterprise, where all the personnel exist *for the sake of* each other, like the organs of the body, with all benefiting when it thrives, just as all suffer when it stagnates (including financial backers). This occurs in spite of the virus of the "class struggle" which the unmoored spirit of the times injects into firms in massive doses, always running into the resistance which the *de facto* solidarity *materially* sets up. Side by side with the family, where the *physical* solidarity of blood and hereditary genes will always withstand the madness of "age groups" supposedly pitted against each other, which the madness of the age tries to inject into the family, private enterprise vigorously defends itself against efforts to create division that assail it. Modern man, inebriated with his autonomy, egalitarianism, and personalism, cannot destroy these last bulwarks that nature erects in the face of his insane dream of liberation without eradicating himself from the face of the earth.

The conditions for the rebirth of the family and private enterprise, starting with their material foundation, also depend on the milieu.

It is certain, in this regard, that the economic vitality characteristic of our times is a favorable circumstance. The pursuit of personal advantage inherent in economic activity does not have the same meaning in a regime of abundance as in one of scarcity, where individual interests diverge even more. When in fact human labor augmented by technology comes to produce more goods than necessary just for the preservation of life, it constitutes a kind of quantitative common good which each person has an interest in seeing maintained and continued, or even expanded. One cannot in effect deny that the prosperity of a nation can be an element of the common good of its citizens who, as they work towards creating it, for the most part unbeknownst to them comply with general justice. We no doubt find there a common good which does not measure up to what we ordinarily understand by the term civilization, yet which still exists; the whole community suffers if anyone, through a kind of Jansenism or puritanism indifferent to the necessities of life, comes to hold it in contempt. The pursuit of material prosperity comes under the scope of the common good which justice orders us to respect. Here are aligned the interest of the individual, for whom the production of material goods is essential, and the duty which is incumbent on man as a social animal. This convergence between self-interest and duty is already inscribed in the structure of economically weak societies, as the wisdom of the fabulist stresses:

> If your neighbor has died
> The burden falls on you.

This holds perhaps to a greater degree in a society that only has at its disposal the basic necessities for life and survival so that it will not give way to total disruption, the end of which is state totalitarianism. Material prosperity clearly cannot be mistaken for social order and civilization, yet it is a precondition for these, as history witnesses.

Nevertheless, of the several conditions which need to be addressed, the first, and undoubtedly the most overlooked, since it is the most difficult to achieve, is the rectification of mentalities.

XXIX
THE FIRST CONDITION:
THE RECTIFICATION
OF MENTALITIES

MODERN MAN HAS entered into an era of economic vitality and technological development while deprived of the wisdom coming from general justice, which influences the conduct of citizens, unbeknownst to them, subjecting their most legitimate personal interests to the good of the whole group in priority order according to their capabilities, gifts, functions, and the duties of their state, which create a bond between them and the group. As long as we fail to understand that the modern age is one in which man frees himself from natural bonds to the world, to others, and to God, it is correspondingly impossible to grasp that the age is *also* one where technology reigns supreme and that it *must* be so out of inner necessity, more powerful than the wills of all. It is *because* man is freed from his ontological forms of solidarity that he wants to transform the world and, in step with his technological prowess, to secure his liberation, not to say to make it complete. Contrary to earlier periods characterized by an economy of

scarcity, but where social (and religious) ties were so
powerful that they obligated those with technical skills
to put their products at the service of all consumers,
our age shows us that the economy of abundance is
the hunting ground for the selfishness of producers
taken individually or in groups. The well-known slo-
gan "the customer is king" has been replaced with the
"reign of producers," foreseen by Saint-Simon.[1] We are
approaching an "era of opulence," with the precon-
ceived ideas of ages of penury without their restraints,
in which "man is a wolf to his fellow man."[2] Beyond
the *de facto* solidarity which the robust economy, born
of technological inventions, establishes among people,
there are superimposed *mental* attitudes based on
antagonism, which physical proximity continually
dispels. The *class struggle* we are experiencing is a
product of the imagination, but the dynamic economy
gives the lie to its existence. Yet its consequences are
only too real and cause it be held as an undeniable fact.

In reality, it is true that human life geared to the
maintenance of production and consumption of
goods is never without difficulties. The distinguishing
feature of material goods is to be *dividable*, and consequently, susceptible to running short or even running
out, if there are fixed quantities and the number of
people increases. In the course of human history over

[1] Henri de Saint-Simon (1760–1825), French political thinker and
social reformer, believed that the most able citizens should organize society for productive labor, which included not only manual
workers but also those involved in trade and the professions.
[2] A proverb dating back to ancient Rome.

the millennia, man has never ceased to be haunted by the specter of famine. This is resurfacing in our times: will not the increase in world population bring this into play in the near, or even immediate, future? They assure us that people will never cease fighting with each other to get their daily bread. They add that the tensions that prevail among them, their antagonisms, conflicts, not to say their inevitable wars, are in the final analysis beneficial. The pressure they bring to bear is a source of vitality. By overcoming them, life restores the equilibrium which is its essence. These tensions are thus indispensable to human existence.

Such reasoning is erroneous and sophistical. If we were to apply it in other areas, we would end up with the astounding conclusion that arguments, even the constant threat of divorce, are factors favorable to the vitality and stability of families! In fact, this logical fallacy is based on the conviction that the economy of abundance is not at all different from the economy of scarcity. Quite to the contrary, as experience shows, prosperity is a positive factor which considerably attenuates antagonisms among people. Lenin, who knew this, taught that the increase of wealth in a society deflects the proletariat from its struggle, and makes it bourgeois. "As long as England is prosperous," he wrote, "there is nothing to be done about British workers."[3] Maurice Thorez,[4] in spite of all evidence to

[3] See his "Letter to British Workers" ((1920) for his analysis of the British working class.

[4] French (1900–1964), leader of the French communist party until his death. See his *La paupérisation des travailleurs français* (1961).

the contrary and with unmatched tenacity, defended the thesis of the "increasing impoverishment of the proletariat." The opposite is true: why this migration to industrial and business centers, to countries with a dynamic economy, if not because one can live there, no longer possible in the place one is leaving? The slums where people somehow or other subsist on the leftovers of the strong economy are worth more, to the one who find himself there, than the land which no longer sustains its owner. *Primum vivere.*[5] It must be said, with Henri de Lovinfosse,[6] that the material goods produced by the dynamism of the contemporary economy become similar to spiritual goods, which are not diminished when they are shared. If there are still a "geography of hunger" and vast malnourished regions, the great famines, which formerly killed entire peoples, have disappeared. If conflicts flare up everywhere, it is often because they are instigated for political ends and to satisfy the thirst for power of ideological empires. The famous Latin American "consciousness raising" is typical here. Far from remedying a reprehensible political situation, it aggravates it, as the example of Chile shows.[7] The tensions buffeting the strong economy do not improve it, far from it, and, if unity is strength,

[5] First live.
[6] Belgian engineer and writer (1897–1977).
[7] Possibly a reference to the socialist regime (1970–1973) of Salvador Allende, in which consciousness raising took a variety of forms, including mass demonstrations, theater productions, protest songs, and the availability of low-priced books published by the government.

disunity is weakness. We cannot hope that unity will be stronger if disunity is introduced into it. In the allegory of the organs of the body and the stomach, Menenius Agrippa has said this better than anyone: conflict among them leads to mutual exhaustion.[8]

---

[8] Agrippa (d. 493 BC), Roman consul, persuaded the plebeians not to secede by recounting this fable, already current in his time, which describes the rebellion of the organs of the body against the stomach, which does nothing but enjoy the food given to it. By withholding food from the stomach, all the organs suffer.

XXX

THE SECOND CONDITION:
SELF-INTEREST AND
DUTY COINCIDE

THIS BASIC OBSERVATION brings to light the second condition. Unity is indeed the principle of all lasting alliances and if one assumes that the people of our time have no intention of regressing to the pre-Neolithic age when the first economic revolution began with the invention of agriculture, it is important to note that consensus is never achieved without the support of the people, and especially without calling into question self-interest.

Pitting self-interest against the public interest has today become a common way of thinking and has moved into many areas of day-to-day activity. How then can mentalities be corrected? Liberal and collectivist political ideas, which divide the world between them, take this conflict of interest for granted. Christian denominations rush to incorporate into their *credos* the doctrine of class struggle and its postulate: from the antithesis will emerge the synthesis and the squaring of the circle, an astounding fallacy which hides the age-old strategy, *divide ut imperes*[1] and the political-clerical thirst for power. Since they are the very ones who in the *social* and *religious* order have the mission of facilitating the pursuit of the common good, they do this while relying on the principle which is directly opposed to it, with the foreseeable consequence that the common good will never be attained. The only solution is to be guided by self-interest, the particular domain of which is the *economy*, and to tirelessly show, through a kind of counter-propaganda and the results produced by the healing of mentalities inside and outside of private enterprise, that it connects to the public interest, *in a dynamic economy*. There is no other means, if the "delusion of opposites"[2] and the irreversible evolution of liberalism towards socialism are to be overcome.

However, it is still necessary for this strategy to adhere to the laws of justice and keep within the bounds of what is permitted by the law. Now general or social justice,[3] which consists in rendering to one's community that which is due it according to the place one holds in the community, is never separated from distributive justice, according to which that which is due to each person depends specifically on the role he plays in society. There is no social justice without a hierarchy in which all the members are ordered, based

[1] Divide and conquer.
[2] Believing two contradictory things at the same time.
[3] Frequently social justice is considered either as an aspect of general justice or general justice with reference to establishing or reforming societal institutions that will contribute to the common good, particularly with regard to the economy.

on their rank, to the common good of the group. An egalitarian society is unattainable and unjust: there is no greater injustice, Aristotle tells us, than treating unequal things as equal.[4] Yet justice is not completely fulfilled if the common good belonging to the group is not apportioned to each person according to the role he has played in the creation of that common good. Society is not a substantial whole, a kind of gigantic individual; it is a whole made up in the last analysis of natural, semi-natural, and organizational relationships among persons. Social justice obligates the citizen to render to each member of the community his due while augmenting or at least maintaining the common good belonging to all. This is to be proportionally divided among all according to their contribution to the common good and the *norms of distributive justice*. St. Thomas writes, "Thus, when a common good is shared among the members of the community, each one receives that which in some way *is his own*."[5] Social justice and distributive justice are inseparable. The common good is the most excellent and most genuine of all particular goods. In it duty and self-interest coincide. In accomplishing the duties of my position, that is, the obligation to serve the whole group in the place I occupy in this whole, I serve my own self-interest.

In a strong economy, there is hardly any problem with the production of material goods, neither with

---

[4] See his *Politics*, 1280a.
[5] A loose citation from the *Summa Theologiae*, II-II, q. 61, art. 1, ad 2.

regard to their quantity nor even their quality. As a whole they constitute a kind of common good. The members of a predominantly industrial society collaborate in the creation of this common good according to the place they occupy in the hierarchy of enterprises and the places those same enterprises occupy in society. This type of common good is inferior to all the others, yet it *materially* unites persons: abundant output is actually impossible without division of labor, allocation of tasks, ordering individuals with respect to each other and uniting them under a single leader with one goal in mind. The common good even unites them formally, in the order of intention, since all have the same interest in making the enterprise, and society, prosperous. The problem is to allocate this good held in common. That is where the difficulty begins: individual and collective egotism which are characteristic of economic activity run the risk here of overturning the order of the common good imposed by general justice, itself inseparable from distributive justice, which functions in the opposite way.[6] If there is injustice in the allocation of the common good, there is at the same time injustice in the creation of the common good, and vice versa. Similarly, if there is justice in the apportionment of the common good, there is justice in its creation, with the reverse being true.

Who determines if there is justice or injustice in

[6] I.e., general justice concerns the duties of the individual to the collectivity, while distributive justice concerns benefits to the individual from the collectivity.

a particular case? Within business establishments, only the manager responsible for the entire firm can effect the allocation of the common good among its members. But in society itself? The stakeholders, the producers? Wouldn't they be both judge and defendant? Wouldn't they be tempted to arbitrarily give themselves the place in society which they think is their due? Wouldn't the *objective* golden mean of justice be surrendered to the conflicts among the *subjective* interests of individuals and groups? How then to ascertain that they have obeyed the prescriptions of general justice according to the duties of their position? If distributive justice is perverted, then so is general justice. This is all too clear.

In reality, the producer is never the same person as the consumer in an economy which is somewhat developed. This is even less the case in a strong economy geared toward a large number of customers, who alone are capable of judging whether or not they have been well-served by the producer. They are really the only ones able to evaluate the products offered to them. No one can do it in their stead. It is a shame that this obvious fact must be noted. The consumers are situated at the end of the economic process. They are the end in both meanings of the word. Production is not for the sake of production, but *for the sake of* consumption. Since the consumers are the ones *for whom* production exists, they serve as the starting point for it: in any activity, the end is the foundational principle, and *judges* the entire process that leads to it. Consumers are thus the judges who determine what place the various producers should have in society, and what their societal obligations are, since they are the only ones who can evaluate the products which the producers offer them and who *pay for them* if they accept them. Commutative justice begins the process of distributive justice and the latter makes known the obligations that each part has, in strict social justice, to the whole.

The three forms of justice are not separate from each other, but complementary to each other. One is never without the others, but it goes without saying that the establishment of social justice, which the state has charge of and which imposes on all citizens the duty to serve the common good, is on account of its preeminence the end of all properly human activities. It follows that the state cannot leave the market, which forges relationships between producers and consumers, to its own devices. Whence comes the third condition. If the proper task of the state is to enforce the law, adherence to which makes the actions of citizens virtuous, in the external forum if not, through a sort of moral capillary action, in the internal forum itself, and if its function is to ensure social justice, queen of all the other virtues, the state cannot tolerate any tampering with the competitive process by the selfishness of individuals and groups, and must be vigilant to see that private interests coincide as much as possible with the public inter-est. The renunciation of this function would really mean suicide for the state. We observe here that total economic liberalism and orthodox communism have the same intention: to completely abolish the state. Now in order to carry out its role of guardian of the public welfare in true justice in a predominantly economic society, which the state itself must obey in order to monitor its application impartially, it cannot be both judge and defendant.

XXXI
THE THIRD CONDITION:
REFORM OF THE STATE

THIS IS WHY THE THIRD CONdition, which will allow the fullest implementation of social justice, calls for the state to get rid of the "fat in the economy" with which it has been endlessly weighed down for decades under the influence of pressure groups. The obesity it suffers from keeps it from doing what it ought to do and sets it to do what it cannot. The state, the guardian of the public domain, cannot insert itself *into* the sphere of the private, which is that of the economy, without becoming a gigantic producer in the face of which consumers, bereft of the power that had delighted them, find themselves impotent. As the state redirects towards itself the ultimate end of the economy, its power, inordinate and inordinately lacking in democracy, is sooner or later appropriated by the most powerful pressure groups, successful in their desire for power. The socialization of the economy is totalitarian by definition, since it involves at one and the same time the public and private spheres, only tolerating man's innermost consciousness on the condition that it be dormant and silent. Getting rid of excess weight will restore to the political power its proper vitality. It will allow it to fix the contiguous boundaries between the public domain and the private sphere.

To this end, the enactment of a *code of regulations for the economy* proves to be necessary, as well as the creation of ad hoc tribunals responsible for the inevitable litigation which arises between individuals or among groups in economic matters, and infractions of laws which have been promulgated. The essential features of this code will ensure that the common good prevails over individual goods, a necessary condition for every society, and that the unity of citizens is protected in the face of the forces of dissolution which operate in every community, particularly when the economic element prevails. It must at the same time preserve commerce from internal and external disruption; this is governed by commutative justice, which serves as a support to general justice, and distributive justice. St. Thomas establishes as a principle that the price of something is in justice defined by its actual value and that this just price is determined by the *common-accepted estimate*, which reflects the judgment of all the members of society, not as isolated individuals, added together one by one, but *as joined together in solidarity*.[1] It is not the fruit of a simple compromise among individuals and groups who are involved together in a transaction, nor of a simple mathematical calculation governed just by the law of

---

[1] See the *Summa Theologiae*, II-II, q. 77, art. 1.

supply and demand. It is determined by a market *the function of which is to be in conformity with norms which are aimed at the good of all and which, far from being based on individual or class interest, are in their application adapted to the common good of society*. The just price and everything that determines earnings, salaries, benefits, investments, tax share, etc. should be born of *unity and strengthen unity*. In the functioning of a given society if one does not begin with this, it is futile to proceed. Otherwise, due to the lack of the antecedent, prerequisite society, there would result a slide into socialism, which never has a human face.

XXXII
SOLVUNTUR OBJECTA[1]

THE OBJECTION GENERALLY made to every attempt to reconstitute society *relying on*—we say nothing more—economic factors prevalent in contemporary life is that material goods are always personal, that their abundance does not resolve the problem. It even exacerbates it; it is pointless to add material goods together, even to infinity, to create the common good, the object of social justice. An argument like this only has any worth for a mind that arbitrarily disassociates man's economic activity from his loftier activities. In fact, and notwithstanding all the efforts of modern economists to isolate economic activity and study it in a vacuum as though it constituted an autonomous system, man's economic behavior is never purely and simply economic, and, even in the most uncultivated individual, material goods are always imbued with a moral dimension. There is no human being who eats like an animal. No matter how far back in history we go, the production and consumption of material goods

---

[1] The objections are resolved.

have always been surrounded with a *religious, and thus social, halo,* as faint as it might be. We must wait for the nineteenth century to see the halos removed, only to be replaced by an ideological nimbus, liberal or collectivist, which aims, though in vain, at giving production and consumption a social purpose, which is already implicit in their connection to other activities, oriented to other people.

If it is true that man is a social animal, this social characteristic cannot be completely absent from his economic activities. The art of living in society has always focused on the reorientation of the intractable selfishness of men towards communal life. The most fundamental society witnesses to this: if the conjugal community had been based only on sexual pleasure, the institution of marriage would never have existed. At all levels of society, the loftier goods which are truly shared by virtue of their spiritual nature, refine and elevate lesser goods which, ultimately, are not shared. It is good for me to have a body—otherwise I would not exist—but this body of mine absolutely cannot be shared. Yet it is from it and through it that the intellect can rise to the properly human sphere of the ability to share.

Though this may be difficult to achieve with regard to material goods, our ancestors had just the same successfully accomplished this on the practical level, since they spontaneously complied with the requirements of social justice, and, even in an economy of scarcity, the forces of unity prevailed over the forces of disintegration. The proof of this is the duration of the Ancien Régime. There is no other option, even in a society where the economic prevails: to restore unity and the common good through the recognition *of its necessity and benefits, if not its advantages, in the most pedestrian and positive sense of the term.* Personal goods are more than ever precarious, unstable, and uncertain if they are not fundamentally linked to the common good. The state without society, without a common good, displays its pomp, always more pretentious and overpowering, which replaces general justice, now vanished. Won't this "cold monster"[2] open up our eyes? What our ancestors accomplished effortlessly, we must do intentionally, lest we slip into "excessive nationalization,"[3] a horrible caricature of social justice, against which Pius XII stood up "to fight uncompromisingly."[4] In the face of the specter of Leviathan,[5] will the instinct of preservation elicit a resurgence of wisdom and lucidity?

[2] A term used by Nietzsche to refer to the state in *Thus Spake Zarathustra* (1883–1885): "State is the name of the coldest of all cold monsters. Coldly it lies; and this lie slips from its mouth: 'I, the state, am the people.'"
[3] *Socialisation* in French, the implementation of socialism.
[4] Radio address to Austrian Catholics, 1952, in which he refers to "the threatening nightmare of Leviathan."
[5] The name given to the state with an absolute central authority by Thomas Hobbes in *Leviathan* (1651).

XXXIII
CHANGING THE SOCIAL
TEACHING OF THE CHURCH

ONE COULD HAVE DOUBTS about this, looking at the evolution of the only moral authority capable of influencing a good many human activities and putting them back on the right path, as it sought to do in the course of past centuries: the Catholic Church. It is doubtful whether the primacy of the common good "more beautiful and divine than the good of an individual,"[1] which was the pillar of the social wisdom of the Church for nearly two millennia, is today acknowledged by the majority of the clergy, from the bottom to the top of the hierarchy. Although it is a constant in St. Thomas and the tradition of the Church to proclaim that "the whole of man is ordered with regard to his end to the whole community of which he is a part,"[2] we are surprised to read in the encyclical *Divini Redemptoris*[3] this incisive and unequivocal expression:

[1] Slightly modified quotation from *Summa Theologiae*, II-II, q. 31, art. 3, ad 2.
[2] Ibid., II-II, q. 65, art. 1, c.
[3] Pius XI, 1937.

Civitas homini non homo civitati existit, "Society is for man, not man for society."

The context undoubtedly adds a significant clarification: "This must not be understood in the sense of liberalistic individualism, which subordinates society to the selfish use of the individual, but only in the sense that by means of an organic union with society and by mutual collaboration, the attainment of earthly happiness is placed within the reach of all. In a further sense, it is a society which affords the opportunities for the development of all the individual and social gifts bestowed on human nature. These natural gifts have a value surpassing the immediate interests of the moment, for in society they reflect the divine perfection, which would not be true were man to live alone. But in the final analysis, even in this latter function, society is made for man, that he may recognize this reflection of God's perfection, and refer it in praise and adoration to the Creator. Only man, the human person, and not society in any form, is endowed with reason and a morally free will."

Similarly, Pius XII declares on September 14, 1952 that "in his personal being, man is not *ultimately* ordered to usefulness in society. On the contrary, the community exists for man."[4] This must be understood in light of the encyclical *Mystici Corporis*[5]: " . . . if we look to its ultimate usefulness, every

[4] Address given to the First International Congress on the Histopathology of the Nervous System, "The Moral Limits of Medical Research and Treatment."
[5] Pius XII, 1943.

moral association of men is in the end directed to the advancement of all in general and of each single member in particular, for they are persons," and also in light of the encyclical *Sapientiae Christinae* of Leo XIII[6]: "Nature did not form society in order that man should seek in it his last end, but in order that in it and through it he should find suitable aids whereby to attain to his own perfection."

As Jean Madiran remarks in his valuable book *Le principe de la totalité*,[7] according to the pontifical magisterium, "society is for man inasmuch as man is PART OF ANOTHER WHOLE, a whole superior to all of society." Furthermore, according to the same author, these papal statements should be read and interpreted within their own perspective: the struggle against modern totalitarianism, unknown to St. Thomas. Society is not a substantial whole, a kind of gigantic individual, whose good, being specific to it, would be extraneous to its members and would be imposed on them from without, as in totalitarian regimes. The human person is not a malleable material which society "puts into a mold," as Mao says, by means of appropriate propaganda for indoctrination and integration into the system, designed to create perfect conformity in mind and action among all citizens. St. Thomas knows that there is a hierarchy

[6] 1890.

[7] Published by Nouvelles Éditions Latines, 1963. See also, by the same author and from the same publisher, *De la justice sociale*, 1961. [Footnote of De Corte's. Madiran (1920–2013) was a French writer and editor of the journal *Itinéraires* for the forty years it was published, to which De Corte was a major contributor.]

of common goods: "Man is not ordered to the political community in all that he is or has.... But all
that man is and has and can do must be ordered to
God."[8] The popes do not wish to say anything else:
God, the common good of the world, is superior to
the common good of the family.

This does not prevent sweeping expressions like
that of Pius XI from giving rise to uneasiness in
the historian of the Church's social teaching and in
the philosopher for whom general justice directs all
virtues towards itself, since general justice alone is
capable, through the unifying power of its architec-
tonic conceptual force, of preventing particular justice,
distributive as well as commutative, from isolating
individuals within their only concern, their own individual good, and of enforcing order, harmony, and
societal peace, which emanate from it and make it
truly just. As Father Louis Lachance[9] aptly writes,
"Politics establishes an order which has the purpose of
forming not individuals, but their actions. It engages
men in just what enables them to come into contact
and collaborate with each other, that is, action. Now
action properly belongs to individual persons, it is
something belonging to them (*actiones sunt supposi-
torum*). It pertains to them as agents responsible for
them ... Thus, if we consider that the specific role of
politics is to direct actions, *we do not see how it might
come to exercise this role unless people submit to it.*
They are the only ones who determine their actions;

---

[8] *Summa Theologiae*, I-II, q. 21, art. 4, ad 3.
[9] Québéçois Dominican historian (1899–1963).

they are the origin of them, the masters of them. If then as persons they are above the political order, if as persons they can refuse the jurisdiction of the state over their acts, we no longer see what purpose a political order could serve ... Politics is practical knowledge having the objective of bringing order to the concrete actions of individual persons. To direct acts, *it must take charge of those at its disposal, that is to say, persons.*" He says further, "*The progress of individuals is not the goal of the organization of life in society, but rather its proper effect.* As it works to produce the general conditions for living well and to put in place the foundations for those conditions, the state is in a position to bring moral pressure to bear on citizens, a pressure *which has as its proper effect to improve them.*"

Our apprehension increases when we read in John XXIII's *Mater et Magistra*[10] that "the permanent validity of the Catholic Church's social teaching admits of no doubt ... human beings are the foundation, cause and the end of every social institution (*singulos homines*[11]— then they are individuals!— *necessarie fundamentum, causam et finem omnium socialum institutorum*)." As one can see, the Latin text is stronger than the French translation, termed official. In *Pacem in Terris*[12] the same pope returns to the same point and even adds a clarification that seems to make the primacy of the person

[10] 1961.
[11] Individual men. The official English translation, closer to the Latin than the French, reads: "Individual human beings."
[12] 1963.

over the common good one of the characteristics of the modern world that he completely adopts: "It is generally accepted today that the common good is best safeguarded when personal rights and duties are guaranteed. The chief concern of civil authorities therefore must *above all* be to ensure that these rights are recognized, respected, coordinated, defended and promoted, and *consequently* that each individual is enabled to perform his duties more easily."

Clearly such a text can only mean the opposite of the social philosophy previously accredited by the Church: now particular forms of justice, distributive and commutative, *are prioritized* over general justice, which imposes on citizens the duty to serve the common good, each in his position, according to his skills and gifts. This reversal implies that the specific interests of individuals and collectivities *are not first governed by social justice* to which they are subordinate and which connects them to the public interest and gives them legitimacy. It is no longer possible to make self-interest coincide with duty if general justice is not *first* respected. This is precisely because the common good and all the possible modes of union in which it consists are commonly forgotten, if not despised, in our day, because "the rights of man" are so often violated that distributive justice works to the benefit of individuals and pressure groups that refuse from the beginning to be parts of a whole with each part in its place. Furthermore, commutative justice almost always sacrifices the interests of consumers, who are the moral end of the economy, to the interests of producers, either competing or in concert with each other. If according to Monsignor Bernard Lalande,[13] international delegate to the international movement Pax Christi and a recognized commentator of the encyclical, "society is at the service of the inalienable rights of the person," it is clear that the society he refers to is at the service of a *dis-society*, since what is personal is in itself incommunicable and unable to be shared. In other words, such a "society" gives the lie to its name. It negates and perpetually destroys itself, and as one must just the same "live" in "society," people will sooner or later be forced to be amassed together as the replacement commodities of society, which is socialism: they will be attracted to this like moths to the flame which consumes them. It is the fate of every kind of personalism to veer towards collectivism. The entire recent history of personalism provides evidence of this.

The contemporary Catholic Church's shift to the left, as it proclaims through the voice of Vatican II that "the beginning, the subject and the goal of all social institutions is and must be the human person which for its part and by its very nature stands completely in need of social life,"[14] similarly makes this clear. As soon as the person is established as the ultimate end, it is impossible to avoid the necessary "stage" of state communism, as Marx himself has said

[13] Priest of the archdiocese of Paris (1910–1998) who assisted in the founding of Pax Christi, a Catholic organization promoting peace, officially recognized by Pius XII in 1952.
[14] *Gaudium et Spes*, no. 25.

over and over again. He too began with the person, whose "self-awareness is the highest divinity," and had the goal of the radical liberation of the person from all the alienations he could fall prey to, in order to fully realize his potential. Yet he was lucid enough to understand that the establishment of the person as the ultimate end of social life requires the intervention of a colossal Power, endowed with all powers: the communist state, capable of completely reversing the course of nature, which destines man to a social life, orders parts to the common good of the whole of which they are the end, and makes their union the condition of all their activities. This is a Utopia in any case, for the "stage" of communism endures, and all the servants of the human person on the way to liberation are quite determined to remain their masters.

Umwertung,[15] the overturning of values traditionally defended by the Church and the primacy of society over the person, constantly professed by St. Thomas, is also emphasized in the pontificate of Paul VI whose attachment to the personalist illusion was reflected in his statements. It logically led him "to prudently crack open the door" to socialism, according to the expression of Lucien Guissard,[16] who wrote the introduction to the French edition of *Octogesima Adveniens*,[17] and "to allow Christians to envisage the degree of their commitment to this path,"

---

[15] Reevaluation, reassessment.
[16] Belgian Assumptionist priest and writer (1919–2009).
[17] Issued by Paul VI in 1971 on the eightieth anniversary of *Rerum Novarum*.

provided they do it with "discernment," according to the term used by the pope himself. Are we then surprised to see a good number of priests and bishops glorify socialism as a panacea, and proclaim with great fanfare that "the implementation of socialism is a grace," or even, in a manner dissembling or bold, going beyond Marxism, "engaging in" the most radical subversion, "cultural" or weaponized? Say what they like, do what they will, their thought contorted in every direction, swinging from *yes* to *no, affirming and denying* the same thing almost at the same time, violating the principle of identity thanks to verbal artifice, there is a consistency, a necessary link between the means and ends: *if the end of society is the person, the means can only be socialism, and it is inevitably substituted for the end put forth.* The history of Anglo-Saxon socialism, born of Methodism, and that of Latin socialism, born of the French Revolution, sufficiently bear witness to this: the philosophy which undergirds both of them is a form of "personalism"; it sets the individual against the existing society and allows him to fully develop in a "new society" which in fact subjects him to the minority which has taken control of power in the state.

XXXIV
HOW INTO BASE LEAD...[1]

OW WAS THIS PRIMACY OF the person imposed while ignoring the most striking facts? For it is an unassailable fact that if I am possessed of a sound mind and true heart, I am not the "origin" of society, still less its ultimate "end." An established society welcomes me beginning with my birth. The society may be worth much or little, but *I did not create it*. The least action of my human nature serves the society around me well or ill: I am not a Robinson, alone on a deserted island, deprived of Friday's comforting presence. In order to live, I need to enter into relationships with others; to live better, union as an end is necessarily imposed on me still more. The parasite itself witnesses in its own way to the social purpose that drives it: the most calculating fop who outfits his personage in front of the mirror does it in view of the social recognition he vainly aspires to attract. He serves society and takes it as an end in his fashion.

---

[1] How into base lead was pure gold changed? From Racine's *Athalie (1691)*.

To establish the person as the beginning and end of society is perhaps only the consequence of an intellectual anarchy which refuses any reality check and feeds on internal representations of its own making, indifferent to whether or not they are in conformity with what exists. This is the reiteration of a concept refuted a thousand and one times by reality and always reappearing in minds turned in on themselves and their dreams. Isn't the person universally the product of society? Isn't he formed by society, and thus more suited to serve it? Isn't it in his greatest, most irresistible interest to impose silence on his mental vagaries and to devote himself to the common good? If we do not choose our bloodline, fatherland, language, or tradition, how could we be the origin of society? *If we love the society of our birth for itself to the point of sacrificing our life for it, how could we be the ultimate purpose of it?* One must have made a frontal attack against the principle of identity and common sense, the highest norms of our intellectual activity, to affirm the contrary as imperturbably as they do in ecclesiastical circles today.

XXXV
HYPOTHESIS:
THE SECULARIZATION
OF THE CHURCH

IN ORDER TO UNDERSTAND THE transfer of rights from society to the person, it is important to develop a hypothesis irrefutably confirmed by contemporary events: wouldn't the assertion that the beginning and end of society is the human person be the consequence of the concept of a supernatural Church brought down to the level of the temporal? Wouldn't this rotation from the vertical to the horizontal itself be the result of an increasing "Protestantization" of minds? It is not a question of treating here the full extent of the subject, which is enormous, but at least of identifying its main features. If it is false to conceive of the primitive Church as being constituted gradually by the personal adherence of each of the faithful to the message of Christ, and if it must be admitted that, far from being a religious organization of purely human origin, the birth and development of which are due to the practical need to unite those adhering to the same doctrine, it has always been, from its origin and from the perspective of believers, the very work of God acting in souls. It is nonetheless true that, if the initiative remains with God, it is composed, not of micro-societies like all societies established by nature and human working, but exclusively of individuals or persons.

We must insistently declare, contrary to the theological liberalism rife among the intelligentsia of all Christian confessions: Christ is the one who "works all things in all" [1 Cor. 12:6], and "He who began a good work in you will carry it to completion when the day of Christ Jesus comes" [Phil. 1:6]. He is thus the beginning, middle, and end of all things, including His Church. The fact remains that the members of the first Judeo-Christian communities were called "saints," that is, those whom God has chosen, those whom He has *called* by their name [Rom. 8:33; Col. 3:12; 2 Tim. 2:10; Rom. 1:6; 1 Cor. 1:24; Rom. 1:7; 1 Cor. 1:2], regardless of the situation in which they found themselves with regard to family, nation, or ethnicity. The Church is, from its origin and forever, the community of persons who are saved (regardless of their social connections) by the salvific will of Christ. Its institutional structure and the functions it assumes are not born of an extension of nature which is strengthened by human skill, nor of a natural need to live in society, but of the love Christ bears towards those He has chosen. It is quite true that Christians are *separated from the world* by their condition of saints and elect and that the primitive Christian community had the feeling of being made up of "strangers," of "wayfarers," "in the middle of a twisted and perverse generation" [Phil. 2:15; 1 Peter 2:11;

Hebrews 11:13]. The city to which they belong is in
heaven [Phil. 3:20]. If Christians are in the world,
they are not "of the world" [John 17:11, 14–16] and
do not belong to it [John 15:18–19] because their end
is elsewhere, in eternity; "the world as we know it is
passing away" [1 Cor. 7:31]. Christ did not come to
save human societies and civilizations, for their very
basis, the marital union, will disappear in the next
life, but to save souls which are always personal and
united to a body which will rise again on the last day.

What binds the faithful to each other is not the
necessities required for life or for a better life, any
more than their free choice to become involved in a
particular community, but *the very presence of Christ*
among those who have answered His call, the presence
of a power both transcendent and immanent which
allows their persons, incommunicable in themselves,
to communicate with each other. This is because it
is no longer they themselves who are the principle
of their acts, but Christ living in them. They thus
form only one body, the head of which is Christ, the
"fullness of Him who fills the universe in all its parts"
[Eph. 1:22–23; Col. 1:18–20]. Such is the Church,
filled with and vivified by a *divine presence*: it is a
society of persons, in contrast to human societies
which are all formed by communities of a lower order
in life, joined together in order to live better. The
sign of incorporation of the believer into the Body
of Christ is baptism, which regenerates the soul and
is therefore always personal. The Church is thus the
only society which is able to be made up of persons

in the fullest sense of the word: *naturae rationalis individua substantia*,[1] that is, of human beings who are not first connected to each other by the necessities imposed by life and the aspiration to live better, but by the irresistible power of grace which draws each of them to the common good. Through Revelation and grace the human soul, incapable of participating in the infinite love of God, is then enabled to obey the salvific dictates of the universal divine justice.

For a society of persons to exist and not break apart due to a turbulent pressure from its members, always naturally prone to withdraw into themselves, it is clear that the Church must wield over souls power similar to that of God Himself: it is, according to the striking expression of Bossuet, "Jesus Christ spread abroad and communicated."[2] This is what the Church is through the doctrine it teaches, the sacraments it provides, the liturgy it celebrates, the holy sacrifice of the Cross, the principle of salvation, which it daily renews on the altar. Now holding power entails the creation of a hierarchy, the promulgation of a series of obligations which guarantee the existence of the one common good, and the inauguration of a juridical order. It is clear, in the eyes of the philosopher who examines this fact without bias, with reason as his only guide, that, without a Church with an established, institutionalized hierarchy, a society of

[1] Individual substances of a rational nature.
[2] Jacques-Bénigne Bossuet (1627–1704), French bishop, theologian, and orator. The citation is from *Pensées chrétiennes et morales*, 1704.

persons would be quickly swept away in the direction
of the disaggregation always threatening "rational
natures" in matters truth, which happens when the
reality to which their judgment should correspond
is beyond their ability to understand. The history
of philosophy has already made this evident in what
could be called "the society of philosophers," since,
always inclined towards subjectivism, their congenital
temptation, they have never ceased to unmake society
over time. As for Protestantism, where everyone is
his own unique church, its division into numberless
sects, and, correspondingly, its relative stability when
there is still an established ecclesial society, are the
historical proof of the law of sociology in question,
from which nothing human or incarnated in the
human can escape.

For the sociologist who has the mind of a philosopher, only a *supernatural* society of persons can exist
and endure. If the Church is involved in temporal
affairs, it is as a supernatural society certainly superior
to all the other forms of society, natural, semi-natural
or artificial, the bearer of *auctoritas* to which every
potestas[3] is subject *in everything that concerns the
order of the salvation of persons*, but with regard to
which this same *potestas* preserves its independence in
what concerns the observance of general justice *and
the two particular forms of justice* which depend on
it, which it has the right to demand of its citizens.
We can then understand the ancient expression of

[3] Respectively authority and power.

Gelasius I, *Duo sunt quibus principaliter mundus hic regitur: auctoritas sacrata pontificum et regalis potestas*,[4] the famous doctrine of the two swords and two societies, each perfect within its own order, and the no less famous thesis of the indirect power of the Church over civil society and its right to judge whenever the temporal order impedes its supernatural mission. It is not a matter of applying philosophy to various analogous forms of the common good, arranged in a hierarchy, which we have already covered: the universal common good, which is God, is superior to the less universal common good of human societies, of another order. As has been written, "in a religious vision of the world where faith holds the first place in the order of values and where it is recommended to work out one's salvation in this world in order to attain eternal life, it is hardly appropriate for the authority possessed of the power of salvation to be effectively in a position of subordination."[5] That would be to subject God to man.

[4] "There are two things by which this world is principally governed: the sacred authority of the pontiffs and royal power," from a letter Pope Gelasius (reigned 492–496) sent to the Byzantine emperor Anastasius II in 494.
[5] From *Les clefs du pouvoir au moyen âge, Jeannine Quillet*, 1972.

XXXVI
NATURALIZATION OF THE SUPERNATURAL SOCIETY

AS OFTEN AS THE BEARERS of sacred authority have encroached on the ruling power in the course of centuries, and vice versa, there can be no doubt that these encroachments cannot be grave *as long as the structure of the ecclesial society does not claim to impose itself on temporal society and vice versa*, and as long as it is not a matter of conflict among individuals or collectivities with a will to power: a society of persons which would replace a society of societies in the temporal domain, or similarly a society of societies which would replace a society of persons in the spiritual domain, would destroy each other. Now if this latter situation has not yet been observed in history, the former has indeed: we even have it right before our eyes, society in the process of breaking down, and, at the same time, of causing the Church to break down. This is the *modern democracy* of the Rousseauian variety, liberal and revolutionary, which has nothing to do with the name it usurps, with a democratic regime, for all time acknowledged by

philosophers as valid in certain circumstances, just
as an aristocratic or monarchical regime is valid in
other circumstances. A political system which claims
to guarantee the salvation of persons in the temporal
order is a recent invention, going back two or three
centuries. It has proclaimed itself as something new
a thousand and one times. However, it is nothing
more than a projection onto the temporal of the
Christian concept of a Church emptied of its congenital reference to the supernatural.

This can be seen. Indeed, if a society of persons can
only subsist in a supernatural God powerful enough
to raise them up to participation in His intimate life,
which unifies them, the knowledge we are able to have
of His revelation cannot be left to the whim of each
individual. There must be a mediator between this
God and man. Since Christ has ascended into heaven,
the mediation of the Church must take His place. The
only way to guarantee the conformity of the intellect
to the divinely revealed reality and the truth of his
faith to the believer is thus the infallibility of the Vicar
of Jesus Christ. Though one may look for it, there
is no other way in the context of a faith which aims
to be fitted to the reality of its object. An organ of
authority *foreign to all personal points of view*, which
guarantees that the doctrine taught by the Church in
its *Credo* and dogma is conformed to divinely-revealed
reality, is strictly necessary *for a society of persons to
remain at the level of the supernatural, its own level.*

There is a supernatural logic just as there is a
logic on the natural level. Their common law is

COHERENCE. If we start from the fact, imposed by history alone, that Christ came to save persons, it is impossible to arrive at any other conclusion satisfying the intelligence. The person, *naturae rationalis individua substantia*, could never develop a representation of the God of revelation, which is beyond his grasp. Who then would guarantee the truth of his representation and its conformity to the revealed God? The person himself? But then that truth would only be based on subject's capacity to affirm something he formulates for himself. It would be irrevocably tainted with subjectivism. The truth of the faith would no longer have God as its principle, but the person in whom truth is seated, and, with its principle in the order of the speculative, its end would be in the order of the practical. From each person having his own truth to his truth being for everyone, there is no criterion for faith other than "lived experience" or "life," in other words a freewheeling judgment, which ultimately corresponds only to an emanation of pure subjectivity, independent of any reference whatsoever coming "from outside" which could constrain it. It is no longer up to the intellect, nor to the will which ultimately supports it, to adapt themselves to the Word of God preserved from all personal interpretation by the authority which Christ delegated to Peter and his successors, but up to the Word of God to subject itself to the inevitable whims of an intellect and will closed in on themselves, cut off from revealed reality. The person becomes his own mediator between himself and the message of salvation.

But as a person necessarily has a rational nature, when its proper object is not God as He is in Himself, it follows that reason — powerfully assisted by the *imagination*, "mistress of error,"[1] its *only* recourse from then on — must *construct for itself*, with the help of bits and pieces borrowed from a dismantled supernatural reality, a mental representation of which it is the principle, which will take the place of the divinity, a representation which no longer has any safeguard when confronted with what is arbitrary. This mental representation originating with the person will obviously share in the temporal character of which the person — *individua substantia* — is possessed: IT WILL NECESSARILY DESCEND TO HIS LEVEL. Where it is widespread, as was seen at the Reformation, the essential objective of which was to destroy the traditional ecclesial institution, the concept of the Church taken as a society of persons sharing the same supernatural beliefs and united under the same head (the Vicar of Christ) will become that of a society of persons, who, WITHIN THE TEMPORAL ORDER ITSELF, will strive to free themselves from all authority superior to themselves. It is thus understandable why Protestant churches, wherever they have triumphed, have given rise to democracies founded on the religious autonomy of the person, soon transformed into political autonomy. If it is fundamentally false to say with Bergson that "democracy is evangelical in essence, and is motivated by

---

[1] From Pascal's *Pensées* (1670).

LOVE,"[2] *it is absolutely true to consider that it was
born of the slow, constant deformation of the concept
of the Church taken as a* SUPERNATURAL *society of
persons directed towards their personal salvation in the
next world, deforming it into a* TEMPORAL *society of
persons aggregated together.* FOR THEIR SALVATION
IS IN THIS WORLD.

Modern democracy is the Church, but as totally
SECULARIZED. This is the reason why it is a RELI-
GION, a religion of the person, a completely *anthropo-
centric* religion, whose goal, conscious or unconscious,
being catholic or universal by way of substitution,
is to eliminate every other religion. To make the
world safe for democracy,[3] this project of Woodrow
Wilson's summarizes the entire logic of the progressive secularization of the Christian religion since
the Reformation. The two *planetary* wars we have
just gone through, which were waged so that the
democratic ideology could triumph, were wars of
religion, for that matter like the wars of the French
Revolution and Napoleon, who sealed for the first
time, with lucidity, according to his own words, "the
alliance between *philosophy* and the saber,"[4] referring
to the rationalism of the eighteenth century, itself the
result of the secularization of the Christian religion

[2] Henri Bergson (1859–1941), French philosopher. The quotation
is from *Les Deux sources de la morale et de la religion*, 1933. After
the quotation, De Corte has inserted: (*sic*).
[3] In English in the text, and mistakenly attributed to Franklin
Roosevelt by De Corte, as previously noted.
[4] The expression is from Hippolyte Taine (1828–1893), French
historian and philosopher.

and its alignment with the world. This is why these wars were unpardonable: they were waged by both sides in the name of the most terrible and voracious of idols: the Self, the person inordinately expanded to the extremes of race, class, or humanity.

XXXVII
LIBERTY

I T WOULD TAKE TOO LONG TO GO into the details of history here, but certainly the revolutionary motto "liberty, equality, fraternity," the glorious evangelical origin of which was lauded by Cardinal Verdier[1] at Prague, the capital of Freemasonry, is the product of the removal of the hierarchical nature of the Church and the secularization of the Church as a society of persons. The dechristianization of Christianity, which has occurred in the course of centuries, has created in the backdrop of Western civilization a *caput mortuum*,[2] a series of Christian concepts devoid of any reference to the supernatural which would bestow meaning on them, which in our time has never been able to be discarded. The religion that is disavowed subsists *in the recesses* of souls. We could demonstrate that all political ideologies which have arisen after 1789 are the product of the descent into the temporal sphere of the supernatural relationship which binds

---

[1] Jean Verdier, PSS (1864–1940) served as archbishop of Paris from 1929 until his death.
[2] Literally "dead head," the expression refers to a useless, leftover substance.

each believer to the divine common good revealed in the Gospel.

"The truth will set you free" [John 8:32], we read in the New Testament: it is what delivers man from sin, uniting him to his Creator and Saviour, and then conferring on him his proper form of being, his person, like to no other, as willed by God; he is freed from all seductive trappings which alienate him from himself and from his origin. Projected onto the temporal sphere, this liberty is then nothing but the liberation of the individual from all the natural common goods that impede the expansion of this liberty and that general justice orders him to respect. Thus, liberty becomes an agent of social disintegration, with an unprecedented power because man, who is the seat of it, always thinks that he is privately in contact with the divinity, which at that point can only be his own person. All the calls for liberation echoing from the four corners of the earth are the proof of this: they are invested with a *mystique*, even the call for sexual liberation and the freedom to abort: if "our wombs belong to us," as was proclaimed on a banner during a march of post-abortion women on the streets of Paris, it is because the person of the woman is *causa sui*, the cause of itself. This is contrary to the words of St. Paul: "You are not your own" [1 Cor. 6:19]. Examples could be multiplied to infinity in other orders, or dis-orders, of society.

XXXVIII
EQUALITY

THE CONCEPT OF EQUALITY before God is subject to the same fate. From the Christian perspective, there is no privilege, right, or particular advantage accorded to one sole individual or to a category of individuals outside of the common law: Christians are all equally subject to the commandments of God and of the Church, to the requirement for baptism and the other sacraments, etc . . . They equally adhere to the same *credo*. They must all equally practice the same religious rites, at least regarding what is essential, etc . . . Thrust into the temporal sphere, this equality demolishes all particular rights of municipalities, regions, recognized bodies, etc. which the Ancien Régime "bristled" with and which created an obstacle to the ever-possible absolutism of the central power. The principle of equality, valid for a *supernatural* society of persons united among themselves by a bond more powerful than any imperative on the natural level, is the most effective element in the destruction of social justice. This form of justice implies, as we have seen, a hierarchy of the parts in relation to the whole, as each

human person is an agent of action in this relationship, and each agent of action is different from the
others from numerous standpoints which differen-
tiate him from others, and, according to the level of
his activity in view of the common good, put him
in the place which falls to him, in strict social justice,
in the community.

It is not at all the same if we transfer the principle of the equality of persons to the temporal social
order: we then arrive at the pulverization of society
into strictly equal atoms, which to hold together
must be kept in place, with the strong-arm tactics of
a central power. This power holds in the temporal
order the place occupied by God in the supernatural
life of Christians: the state becomes the master taking
the place of God, and produces a pseudo-religious
ideology that binds citizens together. It is the head of
a "mystical body" in which divine grace is replaced by
the religion of the "new society," to be built out of
nothing (as the Mystical Body of Christ is built out of
our radical powerlessness to save ourselves) under the
vigilance of the minority of the "super equal," who
occupy the engine rooms of the central power. Social
life is replaced by the mechanization, or, better, the
social petrification, of those who have remained more
or less faithful to revolutionary individualism, which
must stand in for the system of laws and regulations
which had increasingly resulted in spontaneous obedience to general justice. This is what happened in all
countries imbued with Christianity: their power was
increased by all the mystical vitality they drew from

the Christian religion. However, the inflexible, egalitarian democracy to which their dechristianization
brought them hems them in little by little through
an administrative and police apparatus, cumbersome
and costly, which paralyzes their social vitality and
makes them into the caricature of hierarchical social
life which is technocracy.

XXXIX
FRATERNITY

AS FOR FRATERNITY, IT IS hardly worthwhile to emphasize its origin as a debasement of Christianity. Christian fraternity is *exclusively* founded on love of one's flesh-and-blood *neighbor*, with whom we share a common faith and the demands of a life in common. The will of Providence put us into an actual, direct relationship, with supernatural grace remedying the weakness of the person (always inclined to withdraw into himself) as God's presence intervenes between oneself and one's neighbor. This culminates when the love of God, the common good of all the parts placed in relation to each other as required by general justice, is extended to love of one's neighbor understood as a person. "Democratic" fraternity or "humanitarianism" empties this love of its supernatural content, which *alone* enables person-to-person communication. Then love is secularized and projected onto the person, who, in these circumstances, can no longer be understood as such, and finds himself absorbed into an abstract representation of himself, into a "concept" of himself; this merges with the subject himself, who internalizes this concept. Consequently, far from loving others inasmuch as they are others, the subject loves himself. Love for the concrete neighbor is debased into love of something remote and abstract, which is the most hypocritical and odious form of self-love. Moreover, it is in the name of humanity that the most unforgivable crimes have been perpetrated: whoever does not belong to this abstract humanity is subhuman, not a man worthy of the name, to be liquidated on the spot.

This lengthy analysis of the odyssey of the Christian concept of the supernatural in the modern world is necessary in order to understand *how dangerous the contamination of Christianity is for whatever is left of authentic justice and society in the contemporary world*. This contamination is due to democratic, individualist, personalist, and collectivist ideologies produced by the inability of its faithful, clerical and lay, to hold to the vertical dimension of the supernatural. These ideologies strive to destroy every society as well as all true social justice. From the perspective of the philosophy of sociology, which is our own, the famous "opening of the Church to the modern world"[1] with regard to what is specifically modern about it, that is, a debased, degraded, overexcited Christianity, not only leads to the "self-destruction" of the Church itself, but to the sterilization of all the seeds of a social renaissance which could still be extant. If the doctrine and pastoral approach of

[1] Referring to an overarching goal of Vatican II. See *Gaudium et Spes*.

the Church were to change, as indicated by all too many signs, the triumphant "theology of revolution" would be raised *on the ruins of social justice* and would attempt to build a universal pseudo-society endowed with a world government, in concert with political ideologies of the same caliber, erupting from the same source poisoned by its secularization. This government would go from personalism to totalitarian socialism and give free rein to politicians and clerics with an unbridled thirst for power. This would be the irrevocable institutionalization of the worst injustice: tyranny.

As long as the Church does not expel from its bosom the ferment of decay brought about *by its own political heresies*, it is vain to hope for a remedy for the evils plaguing contemporary society. The Church can actually only respect the boundaries separating it from Caesar by rendering to the supernatural God what it proposes to men, the worship due Him. It is not by opening itself to the world and going towards it with full force, a burden imposed on it when it embedded itself in time, but by opening itself to the supernatural, so that natural communities, today attacked on all sides by individualism and collectivism, can be reborn. From the Christian point of view, grace heals nature wounded by man and consequently heals his disfigured social nature as well, but it only does this when it is directed to the only beings able to receive its gift and act in the social arena: persons. It is thus by elevating persons to the supernatural level that the Church fosters their natural social character and their inborn tendency to obey, like parts of a whole, social justice, enjoined on them to ensure *the primacy of the common good*. It will not do this by becoming a "Movement to Promote Universal Democracy Spiritually" (a MASDU[2]), the vesanic[3] temptation which it experiences today. From the strictly sociological perspective which we are considering here, the Church, which, in spite of its state of decay, holds enormous influence, will be able, as it saves persons, to save *the seeds* of the society to come.

[2] Acronym of the French name for this movement. In the literature, the French has been rendered "Spiritual Animation of Universal Democracy." See the work of Father Georges de Nantes (1924–2010), especially *Against the Schismatic Drift*, published between 1969 and 1978. He was an outspoken critic of Paul VI.
[3] Related to insanity.

XL
CONCLUSION

NOTHING WILL BE ACCOM-plished without the slow, difficult, and necessary *rectification of unbalanced mentalities*, victims of an individual and collective subjectivism, seen in the disregard, unsurpassed in history, for authentic social justice and the refusal to see the best of specific goods in the common good, around which all the others revolve. The consequence of this is that men have never to such a degree invoked and glorified "social justice," which then they no longer practice. Social justice has indeed become for them what their lack of it has created: a perennial demand which obligates the state without society or a state at the pinnacle of a dis-society to distribute its free gifts, substitutes for divine grace, on a growing crowd of suppliants, which antagonizes the individual and collective *self*. But nothing costs more than what is free. Thus, one can ask with Bainville whether modern "society" (inasmuch as that word can still be used) will perish because it has cost too much.[1] The appalling wastefulness of states in

---

[1] Jacques Bainville (1879–1936), French historian and journalist. This is an indirect citation from his *Réflexions sur la politique* (collected articles), 1941.

every domain, in peacetime and wartime, is a warning
sign of this, not to speak of the depletion of assets in
every area due to pressure groups and apparatchiks on
either side of the iron and bamboo curtains who divert
power and resources to themselves and their clients.
Inflation plagues all parties. An unforeseen event or
an accumulation of lesser, uncontrollable happenings
is enough for states to collapse or throw themselves
into a new indefensible war in order to get a reprieve.
No matter what one may say or do, inflation cannot
be controlled; it can be remedied only by going back
to what causes it: the negation of true social justice,
which subordinates persons and groups of persons to
the common good of society. It is the soul of society
that is ailing, or, if you prefer another metaphor, it is
its foundation which is shaken to its very depths.

At first glance, as through the most powerful tele-
scope that could probe into the future, we can see
no other solution to the problem, unprecedented in
history, of a society based on economics, into which
we have entered, than the restoration of true social
justice and the vigorous rejection of its caricature.
Moreover, the dynamism which has given rise to
this economic society and which keeps it in existence
necessarily presses it to do this. Indeed, it creates a
de facto solidarity which is waiting to be actualized.
Throughout the dis-society, there is another society
which is forming in response to this call to life. Man,
a naturally sociable animal, slowly makes his way
back up to the surface of the water, swollen by the
torrent of individualism combined with the deluge of

collectivism. The division of labor and the pressing demands of life force him to return, beyond liberalism and Marxism, to perennial social justice, which orders the submission of the parts to the good of the whole and their mutual collaboration. Of the natural and semi-natural communities devastated by a divisive, combative spirit, there scarcely remains anything but business concerns, especially those unaffected by gigantism, a phenomenon of pathological growth and a prelude to the collectivist Leviathan. In spite of all the forces of dissolution which assail them, these enterprises resist the dissension which would mean their death sentence. None of them would be able to survive and function if man's instinct of self-preservation, stronger than destructive ideologies, did not ensure that, in these privileged places, unity prevails over disunity and care for the common good over scorn for it or its parody. Everything happens as though the social nature of man were spontaneously oriented towards *material reality which does not deceive* or towards *an economy where dissension is immediately and concretely penalized* to ensure his welfare. There is, of course, the family, but in the individualist or collectivist "democracy," it no longer has a political role, while the survival of businesses requires disengagement from any spirit of divisiveness nourished by an egalitarian ideology. The hierarchy without which there cannot be a just society survives there, with exceptions, of course, as with everything that is human. Hence reality is stronger than fiction of any kind: the interests of workers, management, and employers come together in spite of everything to safeguard the common interest.

From that point on, philosophy, which is disinclined to play the seer, only sees one possible direction. Knowing that man is an animal who builds civic societies in order to *live better* and that the polity is a society of societies which are themselves ordered to the common good of the whole, it is certain that, to place every business in its proper place in the whole of which it is a part, there remains only well-regulated competition, subject to moral precepts and to the law, with the state exercising oversight. The rest is not under its jurisdiction.

If such a society is reborn, it will be less stable than earlier societies. But none other is visible on the horizon. Moreover, it will only ensure conditions for living better, not living better in itself. But we know from history that economic prosperity in no way contradicts man's contribution to a common good concerned with the practical. We have to begin at the beginning.

We are thus entering into a Nouveau Régime,[2] less glorious than the Ancien Régime, but with the incomparable merit of being in existence. Thus, a true renaissance will begin, a renaissance which will not be, according to the expression of Chesterton, a new fall. Thus, justice, the queen of all the virtues, will be restored.

---

[2] New Régime.